SAILING

BIG

ON A SMALL SAILBOAT

Other titles of interest

Basic Coastal Navigation
Frank J. Larkin

A clearly written, easy-to-understand introduction to coastal navigation. It can be used for self-study or in a course setting, and it also provides a valuable reference for the more experienced sailor who wants to freshen up his skills.

The Boating Bible
Jim Murrant

This handbook contains all the essential information sailors need in one easy-to-use volume. Thorough descriptions are given for all the topics covered. The practical side of sailing is emphasized.

Modern Boat Maintenance
The Complete Fiberglass Boat Manual
Bo Streiffert, ed.

This is *the* book to turn to when dealing with questions of maintenance, improvement, or repair. You will find clear explanations and easy-to-follow, step-by-step instructions covering the fiberglass hull, deck and superstructure, as well as rigging and sails, engines and much more.

Sails
The Way They Work and How to Make Them
Derek Harvey

Contains all the information a boatowner needs to understand how sails work, and how to design, make, repair and modify them. Free computer software is available with the book to help make the process easier.

Something Borrowed
101 Useful Tips for Every Sailor
Joel Graffley

A collection of small refinements and improvements that every owner of a production boat can make to ease living aboard and for more efficient operation at sea. "The handiest sailing tips book ever. . . . full of gems that will keep any cruising sailor busy." *Sailing*

There Be No Dragons
How to Cross a Big Ocean in a Small Sailboat
Reese Palley

". . . a delightful blend of information and stories, with emphasis on the human aspect of sailing. Witty, irreverent, and inspirational with as much 'why to' as 'how to'." *Cruising World*

Sheridan House
America's Favorite Sailing Books

SAILING

BIG

ON A SMALL SAILBOAT

SECOND EDITION

JERRY CARDWELL

SHERIDAN HOUSE

Published by Sheridan House Inc.
145 Palisade Street
Dobbs Ferry, NY 10522

First edition 1993
Second edition 1997

Library of Congress Cataloging-in-Publication Data

Cardwell, J. D. (Jerry Delmas)
    Sailing big on a small sailboat / Jerry Cardwell. — 2nd ed.
       p.   cm.
    Includes index.
    ISBN 1-57409-007-0 (alk. paper)
    1. Sailing.   2. Sailboats.   I. Title.
  GV811.6.C36   1997
    797.1'24—dc21   97-41470
                                                                          CIP

Editor: Janine Simon
Designer: Jeremiah B. Lighter

Printed in the United States of America

ISBN   1-57409-007-0

ACKNOWLEDGEMENTS

I would like to thank Catalina Yachts, Hunter Marine, and Mac-Gregor Yachts for permission to use the photographs of their trailerable sailboats. In addition, West Marine Products have been most gracious in granting permission to use several photographs and drawings of the sailboat products they sell to help us sail big and safely. Finally, I would like to thank my fellow sailors of the Tuscaloosa Sailing Club, in Tuscaloosa, Alabama. Special thanks to Wayne Townsend, Bob Dunn, and Tom Russell; all three know the joys of trailerable sailboat sailing.

Contents

5 *The Challenges*   107

6 *The Necessities*   125

7 *The Amenities* 143

Preface

I do not believe that anything can compare to a warm evening on a sailboat. Sitting in the cockpit after a spring thunderstorm, watching a reluctant sun splash its orange hues on a darkening blue sky, listening to the sounds of the waves, and gazing up at the emerging stars while the moon softly announces that the world indeed continues to be whole, one acquires a sense of personal security and peace that cannot be found anywhere else.

I presume that a fair number of sailors began as I did, looking in the pages of *SAIL, Sailing, Cruising World,* and other magazines and imagining the peaceful feeling of sailing and the tranquility of a night at anchor; all alone on a warm night with gentle breezes, a sky filled with stars and moonlight, and a good book. As I created it in my mind, I would drop anchor in a quiet cove, stretch out in the cockpit with a cool drink, and commune with nature while awaiting evenfall and time for bed in my cozy and secure cabin.

I think I would be safe in venturing a guess that thousands of people have had a similar dream. Unfortunately, the popular mythology surrounding sailing and sailors has led most of these people to believe that they could not afford to realize their dream. That's a pity, because doing so is within the reach of most of the people who think it isn't.

One way of living the dream is to buy a truly small sailboat and "keep it simple." That's fine if you enjoy roughing it in truly cramped quarters, with almost no room to move around. In these boats your chin is always touching your knees, you can never quite raise your head up and, if you want to use the "head" you must order everyone out of the cabin, or into the cabin while you move the toilet to the cockpit. This is what I call "sailing small on a small sailboat." For me, the cramped quarters and sheer discomfort of it all doesn't even come close to fulfilling the dream we share.

Let me assure you, however, that the dream can be fulfilled on slightly larger small sailboats. Rather than buying a 14- to 19-foot "microcruiser," I recommend that you buy a trailerable sailboat that is 22- to 26-feet long, and think big, not small, as you equip it.

My own reasoning works this way: When I was young I sailed microcruisers in total discomfort. It was fun then. It isn't now. However, I won't buy more sailboat than I can possibly afford, a 30- to 45-footer which will cost $80,000 to $125,000 or more to buy and equip. Not me. I'll buy a 22- to 26-foot boat, equip it to sail big, and spend a lot less.

This leads me to Cardwell's First Law of Sailing Big, and it is the premise upon which this book is based—YOU CAN SAIL BIG ON A SMALL SAILBOAT FAR MORE EASILY AND FOR MUCH LESS MONEY THAN YOU CAN SAIL SMALL ON A BIG SAILBOAT.

In the pages that follow, I hope to give you a convincing look at the correctness of this law.

1

The Possibilities

Buying a boat, the right boat for the right person, is a very tricky thing. It is like getting lovers together in the sense that the chemistry is either there or it is not. You have to fall in love with a boat before you buy it, and love being in the air does not make for clear thinking. It is a subtle and difficult problem.

HUGO LECKEY, Floating

➤ AN INTRODUCTORY CONFESSION ≺

It is necessary, I think, to begin with a true confession—I am not a lifelong sailor. I did not have a kind, gentle, and nautical father to instruct me in the fine art of living in harmony with the sea and sailboats. I've only been sailing for 25 years, and all of those 25 years in sailboats less than 30 feet long. But I have sailed in a lot of places, in vastly different conditions, on boats as tiny as the Sunfish, on open-decked sloop-rigged daysailers, on microcruisers, compact cruisers, and 22- to 26-foot trailerable family sailboats. I have sailed on the very cold waters of the small Rocky Mountain lakes, on large inland lakes in the Midwest, TVA lakes in the middle and lower South, and in southern coastal waters. In all of this I have never chucked everything and sailed off to Bora Bora. I have never sailed off to Bermuda, the Virgin Islands, or even Nassau.

I have daysailed a whole lot, and I have overnighted with my wife and two sons on my 19-foot O'Day Mariner on a night when the water in the bilge froze to a solid block of ice! I have overnighted and spent weekends with my two sons on my Catalina

22 more times than I can remember, and I have spent several seven-day cruises along the Alabama and Florida coasts on my trailerable sailboats. It has not all been pleasant; in fact, some sails have been downright miserable. But they have all been worth it. Each sail, whether a daysail, a weekend trip, or an extended cruise, has two essential highlights. One, of course, is the joy of being on the water as part of the elegant natural relationship between a sailboat and the elements of the environment. The second, while more mundane and pedestrian, is no less important. It seems that each time I go sailing I learn about something new that others have on their boat which contributes significantly to their sailing comfort and, therefore, to their enjoyment of the sailboat. Everytime I go sailing I come back with a list of things I need to buy for my trailerable sailboat that will make my next sail a more memorable and enjoyable one. That's what I want to tell you about in this book.

➤ THE VENUE ≺

This is a book about sailing comfortably on a small sailboat. Over the past 20 years I have tried to read every book I could find that was remotely connected with trailerable sailboats. Each of the books has proven to be unsatisfactory in one way or another, primarily because they were written with the assumption that the readers were either offshore bluewater sailors or people who could only afford to daysail or overnight by "camping out" on the water. In the pages that follow I will make no such assumptions. I will not refrain from using the sailing terms I happen to know, although I make no claim to being an "old salt" in this regard. What I will do is inform the reader about the possibilities of doing the type of sailing the "big boys" do, but in smaller boats and in less volatile bodies of water, such as lakes and coastal areas. Permit me to relate a brief example to you.

Picture, if you will, a quiet little marina just off the Intracoastal Waterway on the coast of Alabama. Three Catalina 22 sailboats are about to leave their slips, motor out into a small inlet, and then into the mouth of a fairly large bay which connects with the Intracoastal Waterway. Two of the Catalina 22s are well equipped, with bow pulpits and sternrails, thick cushions in the cockpit, color-coded halyards and sheets, lifelines, VHF radios, sail-control lines leading to the cockpit, and large biminis to shield the occupants from the hot sun on this 90-degree day. The third Catalina 22 has none of these things, save a bow pulpit.

The three boats motor out, and after discussing the matter on their VHF radios, boats one and two agree to point into the wind and raise their sails. At the skipper's request, the crews of boats one and two remain sitting in the cockpit, grab the mainsail and jib halyards, and raise their sails. The skipper points the boat off the wind, they open something cool, and sail away. On boat three, the skipper also heads into the wind and asks his crew to go forward and raise the sails. The crew leaves the cockpit, climbs up to the cabintop at the base of the mast, grabs a halyard and begins to pull. However, because all of the halyards are exactly alike (same color and diameter), he raises the jib instead of the main-sail. The jib sheet is cleated aft in the cockpit; this causes the sail to fill, and the boat's bow to fall off the wind. The boat starts to heel and the crew automatically grabs the mast to steady himself. Finally, after the skipper heads back up into the wind, he locates the halyard for the main, and raises the sail. After cleating the hal-yard he scrambles back into the unshaded, sun-drenched cockpit. Like those on boats one and two, the skipper and crew open a cool drink and begin to drink as sweat pops out on their brows. Because they have no sternrail to lean back on, they sit up straight and sail away.

After four hours of sailing in the bright 90-degree sun our in-trepid sailors in boat three will return with tired backs and ex-posed skin that can best be described as "medium-rare." This is an example, albeit only a brief one, of the difference between sailing "big" and sailing "small" on a small sailboat.

➢ THE RATIONALE ➢

People are attracted to the wonders, the mystery, the challenge, and the pure joy of sailing. Some like the friendly competition of sailing, while others seem to welcome the opportunity for endless tinkering with their boats, even if they seldom actually sail them. Still others own boats to enjoy the quiet, rewarding, and relaxing pastime sailing offers. Most of us, I suspect, go sailing for the pleasure of the whole experience. One thing, however, is clear. Although our attraction to sailing may be as varied as in past years, the boats we are choosing are not the same.

Maybe it's the economic uncertainty or perhaps it has something to do with the demographics of the aging population of baby boomers who have grown wiser, more practical, and more interested in real substance rather than frills. Whatever the reasons, more people are discovering trailerable sailboats as a way to combine their enjoyment of the rigors, excitement, and pleasure of sailing with the economic realities of the present day. Today, the liveliest segment of the sailboat market is in small boats, usually trailerable sailboats. It is clear that the majority of first time sailors are entering through this segment of the market. Not only that, many people who are tired of the complexity, equipment and maintenance costs, crew requirements, and limited sailing time on their big boats are downsizing in order to continue sailing, and to actually do more of it. I believe they are doing the right thing. Smaller, trailerable sailboats are not only fun, they are far less complicated and can be sailed comfortably by a smaller crew. For many of us, life is in great need of a heavy dose of the simplicity these smaller sailboats offer.

When I bought a used Catalina 22 some years ago, almost all of my friends and coworkers made comments like "what did you do, rob a bank?" or they would laugh and call me a "social climber." The fact that sailing can be a reasonably inexpensive sport and leisure activity was then, and still is, one of the world's best kept secrets. Sailing's long-standing reputation for being reserved for the truly wealthy is a product of the days when boat building was very expensive, and before fiberglass made the mass production of light-weight sailboats with swing keels and water ballast possible. More than likely, the media hype and great expense of the recent challenges and defenses of the America's Cup and other big-time sailing events also contribute to the idea that sailing requires a lot of money, and this belief deters many people from trying the sport.

In recognition of this perception in the public mind, Robert Hobbs, then president of the United States Sailing Association, sent a letter to the sailing media requesting the following: "In an effort to increase the appeal of the sport of sailing to the general public and in an attempt to dispel the elitist image often associated with our sport, I would appreciate it if you would refer to 'sailing' instead of 'yachting.' " Interestingly, I once had a status conscious colleague who often spoke of yachting at his summer home, conjuring images in my mind of a 40-foot cruiser. Later, I was amused when I learned that during the summer he did his "yachting" on a little 14-foot West Wight Potter. Of course, like other activities such as golf, hunting, fishing, auto racing, and powerboating, sailing certainly can become quite expensive. But to be honest, it doesn't have to be.

If you are like me and don't have a limitless supply of money but still dream of going sailing, I want to offer what I think are eight very good reasons for buying a 22- to 26-foot trailerable sailboat as a way of living your dream and participating in one of the few remaining leisure activities that can present a challenge, provide freedom, adventure, companionship, and solitude at the same time.

➤ EIGHT GOOD REASONS FOR BUYING A ➤ TRAILERABLE SAILBOAT

Affordability

Reason number one has to do with cost. By affordability I mean that you can buy a trailerable sailboat in the 22- to 26-foot range for *a lot less money* than you can buy a 30- to 40-foot sailboat. For example, a buyer will pay about $550 per foot for a new Mac-Gregor 26X, while a Caliber 30 costs $3,000 per foot. Put another way, for each additional foot over 26 feet, a buyer pays almost $20,000 per foot for the pleasure of a 30-foot yacht. My point is that a lot of very practical people seem to be deciding that the $77,460 difference in cost between a 26-foot trailerable sailboat and a new Caliber 30 translates into the ability to purchase all the equipment one might need to sail in comfort on the smaller boat, with a large amount of money left over to pay for sailing and maintaining the boat for a long, long time (and maybe sending two children to college). As a result of such simple arithmetic, the trailerable sailboat market is growing rapidly.

For used boats the price differences between smaller and larger new boats are the same as with new boats and even sometimes more dramatic. I'll give you a good example of what I mean when we talk about buying used trailerable sailboats. (See Chapter 8.)

Availability

Just three major sailboat manufacturers—Catalina, MacGregor, and Hunter—have combined to produce over 55,000 trailerable sailboats in the 22- to 26-foot range. The large number of these sailboats means that people have a lively interest in this market, and it is likely that even more and different models will be available in the future. And, this also means that if you ever want to sell your trailerable there will certainly be lots of potential buyers out there.

Portability

You can put a 2000- to 3000-pound sailboat on its trailer, hitch it to your vehicle, and head off to new sailing waters every weekend. Try that with a 10000-pound, 32-foot sailboat and you will lose your transmission before you get out of the driveway. If you want to move a 32-foot sailboat over land, you will most likely have to contract with a professional boat hauler to do it and that involves a tidy sum of your money.

If you are still unconvinced about your decision to buy a trailerable sailboat, give this a try: Get a map and draw a circle with a 150-mile diameter around where you live. Now count the number of lakes, rivers, and reservoirs inside the circle. Each one is a different sailing area you can easily reach on a typical weekend with a trailerable sailboat. You can't do that with a 32-footer!

Liveability

A trailerable sailboat has everything you need to live comfortably onboard for several days, or a couple of weeks. Your sailboat is your home on the water. On your trailerable there is a kitchen, a living room or den, a bathroom, and bedrooms. Admittedly these areas are somewhat downsized on a 22- to 26-foot sailboat, but they are, nevertheless, real definable spaces. Combine these areas with the standing headroom provided by a hinged seahood (pop-top), and a trailerable sailboat can be truly liveable.

Sailability

A trailerable sailboat is truly easy to sail, even by one person. On the other hand, it is a basic tenet of sailing that a larger boat means greater difficulty in handling. You and your spouse, your son or daughter, or a friend, can sail a trailerable sailboat with ease.

Because of its forgiving nature you will actually do more sailing on a trailerable sailboat. You can even sail single-handed, something you will be reluctant to do on a 30- or 40-footer, especially if you are new to sailing.

Repairability

Problems on a small sailboat tend to stay small, and big problems on a trailerable sailboat are smaller than small problems on a big sailboat. Masts and booms are shorter and lighter, sails are smaller and easier to handle, running aground is simpler to deal with, and the boat is easier to sail in light winds. This is no trivial matter, because small problems are easier to fix than big ones. Broken parts on a trailerable sailboat are certainly less expensive to repair than broken parts on a big boat, and that leaves you with more money for having fun with your boat. After all, isn't that the point?

Raceability

If you are the competitive type and want to participate in racing, a trailerable sailboat is what you want to own. Wherever you find trailerables, you will find them racing against each other— whether on lakes, rivers, or along the coasts of America. It's easy to load the boat on its trailer and head off to the race that's being held by a sailing club 250 miles away. That is out of the question for bigger, nontrailerable sailboats.

Cruisability

Finally, there is what I call cruisability. If a boat is affordable, easy to take places, simple to sail, easy to fix, and comfortable to stay on, it is more likely to be used, and used often. Of course, if you will only be fulfilled by sailing off to Bora Bora or battling with the winds and seas around Cape Horn, trailer-sailing is not for you. If, on the other hand, you have the desire to use your own skills and abilities to get your sailboat from one place to another over a three- or four-day period, a trailerable sailboat is all that you need. One of these sailboats can take you to new and exciting places that are reachable for a few days of getaway and exploration. On each trip you will meet new people, explore new coves and sloughs, and learn more about your boat and yourself.

You can cruise with great ease on a trailerable sailboat. Just like on the big boats, you can keep cool, lounge around, light up the cabin, and keep clean. You can sleep in comfort, swim with confidence, and watch television or listen to some good music. You can grill out, knowing where you are going and letting an auto-pilot help you get there. You can know the depth of the water in which you are sailing or anchored and, of course, you can keep in touch using your VHF radio. In other words, on a trailerable sailboat you can cruise in comfort and safety.

I think you will have made a very good decision if you buy a trailerable. You will not only be able to pay for your trailerable sailboat, but because of its user friendly size, you'll actually go sailing on it.

If you want your sailboat to be a status symbol, a trailerable sailboat is probably not for you. If, on the other hand, you want to go sailing, if you want to do so with relative ease and in accept-able comfort without worrying about year-round slip fees, costly maintenance, and huge boat payments, a trailerable sailboat may be just the ticket. I invite you to give it a try.

➢ A QUESTION OF DEFINITION ≺

For some reason if a boat is capable of being trailered behind a well-powered family car or van, it is called a "small" sailboat. Practically speaking then, a Catalina 22, a Hunter 23, or a Mac-Gregor 26 is a "small sailboat." The notion of "small" is an inter-esting concept. When we were living in Bowling Green, Kentucky, we owned an old English Tudor house with a living room that was 25 feet long. One winter afternoon I stood at one end of that room and imagined a sailboat that was as long as from where I was standing to the other end of the room. I invite you to do the same. If your living room isn't that long, step off 25 feet from a tree outside to get a feel for what the distance will be from bow to stern on a 25-foot sailboat. You will agree that the distance doesn't seem to be compatible with the word "small." Be that as it may, most sailboats over 25 or 26 feet have beams (maximum width) over eight feet and require a special permit on most high-ways. As a result, the boats we will consider in this book are re-stricted to the 22- to 26-foot range. Let's take a look at some of the basic properties of the sailboats that fall into this category.

➢ TRAILERABLE SAILBOAT BASICS ≺

As you probably know, or could easily guess, there is a good va-riety of 22- to 26-foot sailboats on the market today. Before we discuss a few of these boats, let's examine some of the various parts of a typical trailerable sailboat and familiarize ourselves with their nomenclature. As we do so, refer to Figure 1-1.

The Hull

The part of the boat that sits in the water is called the *hull*. Two appendages also extend from the boat into the water—the *keel* or *centerboard,* which is usually an integral part of the hull, and the *rudder,* which may or may not be attached permanently to the hull. As you can see from Figure 1-1, some boats have keels that are permanently fixed in place and extend two to four feet below the hull, while others have what are called "swing keels" that can be raised and lowered. On some trailerable sailboats like the Mac-Gregor 26, the centerboard retracts all the way into the hull, thus allowing the boat to maneuver in very shallow water.

The painted or molded-in stripe that runs around the lower part of the hull above the underwater sections is called the *boot-top*. At the bottom edge of the boot-top is the boat's *waterline.* The waterline defines the water level on the hull when the boat is float-ing on her designed lines, as delivered from the manufacturer. The *gunwale* (pronounced "gunnel") is where the deck joins the hull. Often there is a rubrail that helps hold the hull-deck joint together. Trailerable sailboats are usually made up of four distinct fiberglass parts—the hull, the hull liner, the deck, and the deck liner. The hull

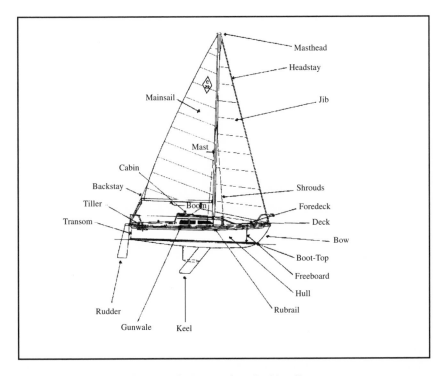

Figure 1-1. Basic parts of a trailerable sailboat

and hull liner and the deck and deck liner are typically fiberglassed together to form a rigid structure, and then the hull and deck are joined together at the gunwale.

The area of the hull between the waterline and the gunwale is known as the *topsides,* and the height of the topsides is called the *freeboard.* Other factors aside, the higher the freeboard the less likely you will be to get really wet when sailing the boat flat on its bottom. The more you add to the boat to enable you to sail big, the more weight you are adding and the more you reduce the freeboard. I have a friend who has so much stuff on his Catalina 22 that the waterline is actually a little under the water. I have sailed with him several times and I can report that the extra weight doesn't seem to affect the performance of his boat, and his boat is the "biggest" sailing Catalina 22 I have ever been aboard.

The Deck

The flat surfaces inboard of the gunwales are considered the *deck*. The area of the deck between the point of the bow and the front of the cabin trunk is called the *foredeck*. On most trailerable sailboats you will notice that the edge of the deck is raised a little, usually about an inch. This part of the boat is called a toerail, and is designed to warn you that you are approaching the edge of the boat by causing you to bump into it with your toes.

Immediately behind the foredeck area is the *cabin,* within which most of the onboard living takes place. The cabin comes in a wide variety of configurations and we will talk more about it in Chapters 3 and 4. Behind the cabin is the *cockpit.* This is an extremely important area of the boat and we will have much more to say about this area of the deck in Chapter 3.

The Standing Rigging

Perhaps the most obvious thing about a sailboat is the large spar projecting high into the sky above the deck of the boat. This particular spar is called the *mast.*

The mast is a spar to which the mainsail attaches and on which it is run up, or raised. On today's trailerable sailboats the mast is made of extruded aluminum and serves other functions in addition to holding the mainsail. We will get to those other functions in just a little while.

As Figure 1-1 illustrates, the mast is held in place by wires called stays and shrouds (sometimes called "sidestays"). The headstay attaches at the masthead and to the stemhead fitting on the bow of the boat, while the backstay runs from the masthead to the stern. The head- and backstays keep the mast upright forward and aft. The shrouds keep the mast from falling to the left (port) or right (starboard), and enable the sailor to orient the mast down the center of the boat. The shrouds are rigged through the ends of rigid spreaders, which are attached to the mast high above the deck level, and which give the shrouds effective mast-support angles. The stays and shrouds are made of stainless steel and are adjusted by turnbuckles.

The boom attaches to the mast by way of a gooseneck fitting and the foot of the mainsail attaches to the boom. Together the mast, boom, spreaders, stays, and shrouds are known as the standing rigging.

Earlier I suggested that the mast serves other functions as well as holding the mainsail. Many trailerable sailboat masts are delivered with masthead lights for sailing at night or for use when at anchor. Others have spreader lights or mast-mounted deck lights to illuminate the boat and aid in moving about when it is dark. Most boaters will have a Windex or other apparent wind direction indicator mounted at the top of the mast to aid in keeping sail-shape when underway. Many sailors attach the antenna for their VHF radio high up on the mast to increase their transmission and reception ability. This is particularly helpful since the VHF signal is a "line-of-sight" signal and will not bend over the horizon. In addition, if you sail out in the open water the mast is often used to mount radar reflectors, which enable other vessels to "see" you on their radar. All in all, the mast on a trailerable sailboat can be home to a host of devices which contribute to safety, convenience, and comfort.

The Running Lights

Today, almost all trailerable sailboats in the size range we are talking about are delivered with running lights installed and ready to use. On the boat itself, there are three running lights, which must be turned on at dusk. Two of these running lights are the port and starboard bow lights; the port bow light is red (like port wine) and the starboard one is green. If you are approaching a sailboat at night and you see a red running light ahead, you know that you are to its port side. The other skipper will see your starboard running light and know that he is on your starboard side. A third running light is white in color and is mounted on the stern of the boat. Thus, if you are sailing at night and you see a white light coming closer, you know you are overtaking another boat from behind. If, on the other hand, you see a white and a green light coming closer, you know you are overtaking another boat from slightly behind its starboard side. Running lights are extremely important and you should make certain that they function well, are good and bright, and meet all Coast Guard requirements.

➤ THE SAILBOATS ◄

Today's trailerable sailboat is a marvel of design, engineering, and construction. That's not surprising because companies involved in the manufacture and sale of trailerables must address several problems if they are to succeed in this segment of the sailboat market. First is the problem of weight; this is especially true today as automobiles, trucks, and vans—both foreign and domestic—are becoming smaller and less powerful. The majority of cars sold in this country are not designed to tow 4000 or more pounds of any-thing, not to mention a sailboat. A second problem area is the ease, or lack of it, in setting up the standing rigging and raising the mast. And finally, a third problem revolves around how to design a small, lightweight sailboat with sufficient room and accommo-dations for limited cruising. These are daunting engineering and design problems.

About the only thing that manufacturers can do to make boats both strong enough to be safe and light enough to be towed behind a conventional vehicle is to build them out of plastic. Just imagine how heavy a 26-foot sailboat would be if it were made out of metal, or constructed of wood strong enough to provide the struc-tural integrity needed to withstand the loads the wind and sea can place on a sailboat. Luckily, fiberglass laminate has the character-istic of being very strong and at the same time, relatively light. Fiberglass laminates can take up to 2500 pounds of force per

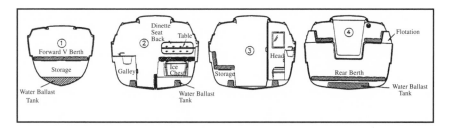

Figure 1-2. Water ballast system on the MacGregor 26X

square inch before failing. It is easy to understand, therefore, why fiberglass is used to manufacture almost all of today's modern trailerable sailboats.

Prior to 1985, the manufacturers of trailerable sailboats used heavy lead, iron, or some combination of these materials with fiberglass to make "swing keels" which provided lateral stability for their boats and permitted them to be loaded onto trailers. In addition, lead was added in the bottom of the boat as ballast to provide additional stability, and this of course negated the gains made with lightweight fiberglass. The problem was how to continue to ensure the stability that ballast provides while reducing the weight lead and iron add to the towing load of trailerable sailboats.

To deal with this problem, the MacGregor Yacht Corporation introduced in 1985 the first water ballasted sailboat made in this country. Called the MacGregor 26, this trailerable sailboat has a large water ballast tank molded into the hull which can be flooded with sea water for use as ballast. Figure 1-2 shows the manner in which the water ballast tank is molded into the hull as an integral part of the sailboat.

When the boat is launched into the water, a small valve is opened and the molded-in tank is gravity-filled with 1200 pounds of water. When the tank is full the valve is closed, trapping the water. After sailing, the boat is floated onto the trailer, the valve is reopened, and as the boat is pulled up the launch ramp the 1200 pounds of water are drained, leaving a remarkably light boat and trailer that can be towed easily.

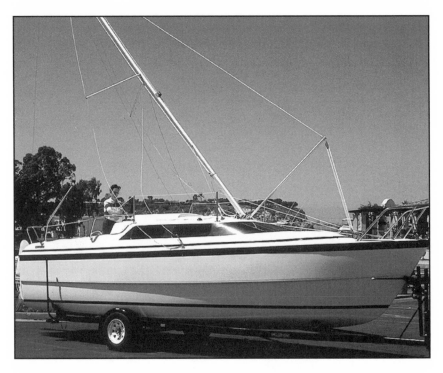

Photo 1-1. The mast raising system on the MacGregor 26X in use

A second significant advance has come in the various systems the boat builders have devised to assist the trailer-sailor in raising the mast. Almost all of these systems use some combination of block and tackle in conjunction with the existing winch system on the sailboat. MacGregor claims that a young child is strong enough to raise the mast when assisted by the optional mast-raising system the manufacturer provides. Photo 1-1 shows the mast-raising system on the MacGregor 26X in use.

➢ BASIC CHOICES ≺

One of the interesting things about life is that we are often required to make decisions that seem on the surface to be quite arbitrary but which, upon closer examination, have some rational basis. I mention this widely known but poorly understood fact of human existence as a preface to introducing my criteria for including, or not including, certain trailerable sailboats in this discussion. My criteria may appear arbitrary, but in fact they are systematic. For the purposes of this discussion, the boats should:

1. Weigh 3000 pounds or less;
2. Have beams (maximum widths) of not over 8.6 feet;
3. Have a maximum length overall (LOA) of not less than 22 feet and not more than 26 feet; and
4. Have a price range of $10,000 to $20,000 for the production model of the boat.

The width of the trailerable is important because as manufacturers have begun making their trailerables lighter by using water ballast, they have had a tendency to use the lighter weight to increase the size of the beam in order to give their boats more interior living space. You should be aware that sailboats with beams over eight feet require a special permit to be trailered over roads and highways in many states (such as New York, Missouri, Pennsylvania, Oregon, Illinois, and Arizona). All states require permits for pulling loads over 8' 6" over their roadways. You need to know the law in the states where you will take your sailboat and make certain you have a permit, if needed. While you may not be caught if you don't have the appropriate permit, you can bet that questions will be raised about the width of your boat and the proper permit if you have an accident. Of course, the manufacturers also know about the width restrictions in the various states.

As I mentioned earlier, in addition to the regulations regarding maximum towing widths, there is the practical problem of boat weight. It is a simple fact that when fully loaded and combined with the weight of a trailer, boats that weigh over 1.5 tons are really taxing on today's smaller and lighter cars and vans. Thus the rationale for the 3000-pound limit. Manufacturers also know about the relationship between the weight of a boat and the stress on the towing vehicle—they just choose to ignore it in some cases, but you shouldn't.

There are, I might add, a number of boats in the 22- to 26-foot range that cost substantially more than the $20,000 limit I have set, with the Nonsuch 26 being one example. It is a fine boat, but it is priced more like a 30- to 35-footer. In addition, it falls way outside of my weight limitation. Finally, if one surveys the current trailerable sailboat market with an eye toward locating boats large enough to offer the possibility of sailing big and yet meeting the other criteria, it turns out that nearly all of them fall into the 22- to 26-foot length category.

Here is my list of boats which satisfy these parameters:

1. Catalina 22markII
2. Catalina 250*
3. Hunter 240*
4. Hunter 26*+
5. MacGregor 26X*
6. Santana 2023*
7. Precision 23
8. Beneteau First 235
9. Seaward 22, 23
10. Jeanneau Tonic 23
11. Com-Pac 23
12. Capri 26

* indicates a water ballast tank
+ Indicates the beam exceeds 8' 6" but is still sold as trailerable

Space limitations make it impossible to review each boat in detail, so I will restrict my discussion to the Catalina 22markII, the MacGregor 26X, the Hunter 240, and the Catalina 250. Note that the other eight boats are also fine products, and deserve investigation.

The Catalina 22markII

The Catalina 22 is probably one of the most popular trailerable sailboats ever built. As an index of just how successful this boat has been and continues to be, over 16,000 Catalina 22s have been built and sold. Quite frankly, that is a phenomenal success in this

Photo 1-2. The Catalina 22markII

market. The reasons for this success are fairly simple, and we will examine them in due course.

Catalina Yachts introduced a new model of the Catalina 22 (called the Mark II) in 1995. While the boat retains the same design for the underwater surfaces, standing rigging, and sailplan, the topsides and interior have been completely redesigned, resulting in an additional eight inches of beam and more walking room between the cabin house and the gunwales. Everyone I have talked to about the new design, without exception, expressed the opinion that they prefer the earlier model. Frankly, the Catalina 22 had become the only classic among all of the trailerable sailboats on the market, and I simply cannot understand why they fiddled with it. However, if you are not familiar with the previous model, the new Catalina 22markII may be just what you are looking for when considering price and other factors. Following are the boat's vital statistics.

The Catalina 22markII is produced with three different keels—a retractable (swing) keel, a fin keel, and a wing keel. The standard boat comes with a retractable keel; if you want either a fin or a wing keel it will cost you a good bit more. Other than the three keel configurations, all Catalina 22markIIs are produced alike.

PRINCIPAL SPECIFICATIONS

Length Overall (LOA)	21' 6"
Waterline Length (LWL)	19' 4"
Beam	8' 4"
Sail Area (Main and Jib)	205 sq. ft.
Mast Length	25' 0"
Displacement (Minimum)	2290 lbs.
Draft, retractable keel up	2' 0"
retractable keel down	5' 0"
fin keel	3' 6"
wing keel	2' 6"
Fresh-water Capacity	5 gal.
Fuel Locker	6 gal.

What You Get. The Catalina 22markII comes with a lot of standard equipment that is often optional on other comparable sailboats. Here is what you get if you buy the standard Catalina 22markII at its base price:

Standard Boat and Equipment: Catalina 22markII
1. The boat with molded-in sheer stripe, boot-top, and non-skid surfaces on the deck
2. Molded-in anchor locker in foredeck, cockpit locker, fuel locker, and opening forward hatch
3. Stainless steel bow pulpit and stern pulpit
4. Molded-in toerails
5. Anodized aluminum mast and boom with internal halyards led aft to the cockpit
6. Mainsail and 110% genoa

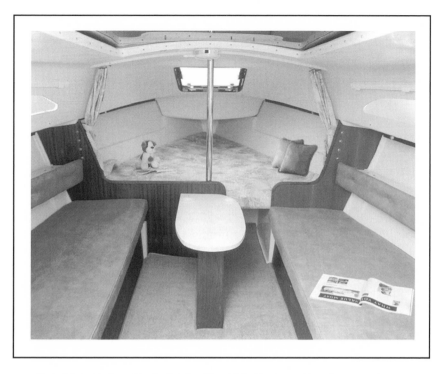

Photo 1-3. Inside the cabin of a Catalina 22markII, looking forward from the companionway

7. Mainsheet traveler with adjustment system
8. Genoa tracks and blocks on adjustable cars
9. Running lights
10. Pop-top cabin
11. Jiffy reefing on boom
12. Boom vang
13. Teak interior trim
14. Ice chest
15. 12-volt D.C. electrical system with control panel and marine battery
16. Interior lights

Photograph 1-3 gives you a view of the interior of the cabin on the MarkII, looking from the cockpit through the companionway. The first impression one gets is that the cabin is rather open, and thanks to the use of teak, not completely stark and white. The cabin not only appears to be wider than the older model, it actually is—by about 10 inches. Notice that a number of optional accessories are shown in this picture: interior carpet, privacy curtains for the V-berth and head area, and cabin window shades. Also note that the cabin sole (floor) is fairly wide and open, with no centerboard trunk intruding. There are settees on the port and starboard sides, with the backrests serving as fiddles for the large shelves behind them. I really like these shelves because they can keep a lot of stuff off the settees. In this photograph you can also see that the cabin table is not movable. If you are as tall as I am (6' 3"), more than likely your knees will not fit under the cabin table. The stainless pole running from the cabin ceiling, down behind the port V-berth bulkhead, is the mast-step compression post. Just like on the older model Catalina 22, I wish it were encased in wood. Behind the port bulkhead is a space for a chemical toilet. While the toilet area is not enclosed, the optional privacy curtains can be used to close off the area. The privacy curtain can also be used to close off the V-berth area located under the foredeck. There is an insert that can be placed in the V-berth to make it large and comfortable. The only problem here is that the V-berth filler boards and cushions cover up the chemical toilet. If you awaken in the middle of the night with an urgent need to use the facility, you must first remove the cushions and filler boards. This process must be reversed upon returning to the V-berth for sleeping. Happily, there is good interior lighting in the V-berth area. Finally, at the forward end of the cabin you can easily see the large, tinted plexiglas hatch which lets in light and opens to allow good circulation inside the cabin.

Photo 1-4 shows the interior looking toward the rear of the cabin from the V-berth area. The cushions for the port settee extend well under the cockpit, providing plenty of legroom when used as a berth. The optional movable galley somewhat restricts the legroom available for sleeping on the starboard settee. You can see the galley in the pulled-out position toward the rear of the cabin on the starboard side. When not in use it slides back, out of the way. The unit is self-contained and includes a fresh-water sink,

Photo 1-4. Inside the cabin of a Catalina 22markll, looking aft from the V-berth area

butane stove, cutting board, and storage compartment. The large ice chest, which also serves as a companionway step, can be seen in the center of the boat. The companionway is of adequate size for entering and leaving the cabin, and the four recessed windows provide good sunlight into the main cabin. The interior of the boat has molded-in fiberglass-lined compartments located under the settees for storage. The galley also has a small storage area.

The cockpit has two opening lockers. The port locker is for holding a gas tank for the outboard motor, while the starboard locker provides access to storage for larger items. In addition, there are drain holes through the transom above the waterline to make the cockpit self-bailing.

I once owned an older model Catalina 22 and spent several

nights on board with my then 17- and 15-year-old sons. We were comfortable enough to want to do it time and again. With a little work, and some important options added, the Catalina 22markII can be made into a really big trailerable sailboat.

With the Mark II, Catalina continues its tradition of producing well-constructed trailerable sailboats. It remains an attractive vessel with traditional lines. Because of its performance, especially when properly equipped, and its ability to hold its value, I give it high marks and recommend it as a top choice for sailing big on a small sailboat.

The MacGregor 26X

The MacGregor Yacht Corporation has been building trailerable sailboats for well over 25 years. In fact, MacGregor pioneered the

Photo 1-5. The MacGregor 26X

retractable keel, a development which made the construction of trailerable sailboats practical. For a number of years MacGregor produced three different sizes of trailerable sailboats—a 21-, a 22-, and a 25-foot boat. While MacGregor has not been noted for building sailboats with a lot of amenities, it nevertheless has been very successful at selling the boats—well over 25,000 of their three sizes. I have never met an owner of one of their boats who was not completely happy with it.

In the mid 1980s, MacGregor decided to devote its energy to the design and manufacture of only two boats, both with water ballast systems—the MacGregor 19 (a combination sailboat and powerboat) and the MacGregor 26 (a sailboat). Once again, as with the swing keel, MacGregor pioneered a new development in American trailerable sailboat construction by the introduction of a water ballast system. The MacGregor 26 proved to be just as successful as its predecessors. In fact Catalina, Hunter, and Schock have all begun producing their own version of water ballasted trailerable sailboats.

In 1995, MacGregor completely redesigned the 26 and introduced it as the 26X. The company took what it had learned from the powerboat features of the MacGregor 19, combined it with what it had learned from the earlier model 26, and developed a boat that they claim doubles as both powerboat and sailboat. According to the manufacturer the MacGregor 26X "offers high speed powering without compromising sailing performance. You can have the peace and quiet of sailing, or the fun of powering around at a good clip— over 24 mph." As a father of two sons, I can remember that when they entered their teens they, like the rest of their friends, found going fast to be more exciting than going slow. I mention this to suggest that the powerboat feature of the MacGregor 26X may serve to keep your teenage children interested and to maintain boating as an activity for the whole family.

Like the older model MacGregor 26, the new 26X derives much of its stability from its water ballast system, and not from a keel or lead ballast. In fact, the MacGregor 26X has a centerboard that weighs only 25 pounds and can be retracted completely into the hull. This permits the boat to sit very low on its trailer, which makes it significantly easier to launch and retrieve than other boats of comparable size. The shallow underbody is also a boon to maneuvering and beaching. The dry 26X weighs 600 pounds more than the older model 26, and uses an additional 300 pounds of water in its ballast tank. This means that when you are pulling the boat out of the water the new boat weighs almost half a ton more than the older 26, and once out, your car will be pulling 600 additional pounds. The MacGregor dealers tell me that much of this new weight comes from an additional layer of fiberglass laminate that was added to absorb the pounding and reduce the vibrations on the hull that occur when the boat is being powered at high speeds. Let's take a look at the numbers on the MacGregor 26X.

PRINCIPAL SPECIFICATIONS

Length Overall (LOA)	25' 10"
Waterline Length	23' 0"
Beam	7' 11"
Sail Area (Main and Jib)	281 sq. ft.
Mast Length	28' 0"
Displacement (dry)	2250 lbs.
Water Ballast	1500 lbs.
Trailer Weight	710 lbs.
Draft, board up	1' 3"
board down	5' 4"
Fresh-water Capacity	10 gal.
Fuel Capacity	18 gal.
Engine Capacity	5 to 50 h.p.

What You Get. In the first edition of this book I commented that the MacGregor 26 comes with a list of standard equipment that is less substantial than the Catalina 22 when you buy the standard boat at its base price. With the new MacGregor 26X, that is no longer accurate.

The MacGregor 26X is manufactured with a white hull, black sheer stripe and boot-top, and molded-in nonskid surfaces on deck. You have no choice in color selection. The MacGregor 26X is much like Henry Ford's famous Model T: "You can have any color you want, as long as it is black." Keep in mind that Mr. Ford's Model T did become the standard for the industry. Here's the standard MacGregor 26X:

Standard Boat and Equipment: MacGregor 26X

1. The boat with molded-in sheer stripe, boot-top, and non-skid surfaces on deck
2. A custom trailer
3. Bow pulpit, stern railings, and lifelines
4. Molded-in toerails
5. Anodized aluminum mast and boom
6. Mainsail and working jib
7. Running lights and masthead light
8. Galley with fiberglass sink, manual pump, tile surface, and 2.5 gallon fresh-water container
9. Space for a stove
10. Removable 48-quart ice chest
11. Marine battery and switch panel
12. Built-in outboard and motor well
13. Interior lights
14. Fabric on seats and berths
15. Wheel steering with pedestal
16. Mast carrier
17. Genoa fairleads
18. Interior carpet
19. Enclosed head area, with sink, 2.5-gallon water system, and mirror
20. Dinette table
21. Foam flotation
22. Molded-in anchor locker in foredeck, cockpit locker, fuel locker, and opening forward hatch
23. Walk-through transom
24. Up to 50 h.p. outboard motor

Photo 1-6. Inside the cabin of a MacGregor 26X, looking forward from the companionway

Although the exterior profile of the Catalina 22markII is more pleasing to the eyes, I want to tell you that when I'm aboard the MacGregor 26X I get the feeling that I am on a boat that is much larger than 26 feet. It is a feeling I find difficult to describe, but it is the same feeling I get when I am aboard the old model Catalina 22 that is, unfortunately, lost on the Mark II. For me, the interior layout of the MacGregor 26X has a big boat "feel," whereas the new Catalina 22markII gives me the sense of being inside a small, fat boat. Let's take a look at the MacGregor and you can make up your own mind.

Photo 1-6 shows the cabin looking forward from the companionway. On the starboard side you can see the dinette table with facing seats, and the settee on the port side. Also on the port side, immediately across from the aft dinette seat, is the free-standing galley. I really like this arrangement because you can actually stand up and prepare food. The galley has a fiberglass sink (I wish it were stainless), a tile counter, and space for a two-burner stove. (The stove shown is optional.) There is a large storage cabinet immediately below the galley, as well as outer compartments designed for small items. You can't see it in the photo, but there is a 48-quart ice chest under the rear dinette seat. There are storage compartments under every seat and berth. Under the foredeck is the large V-berth with a good-sized opening hatch immediately above. The large stainless steel pole running from the cabin ceiling alongside the dinette table is the mast-step compression pole. Just like on the Catalina 22markII, I wish it were encased in wood. The boat is fully carpeted. The cabin has six large windows which let in a lot of light and create a sense of space. Finally, the dinette table can be lowered to convert into a double berth. The back of the forward dinette seat lifts out to create a sleeping area that is 13 feet long. Although the manufacturer calls this a double berth, I think it is more a single berth designed for one large adult, or a double berth for a small adult and a small child.

If you stand in the V-berth area and look aft, the first thing you will notice is the very large companionway for entering and leaving the cabin. For someone my size, this is truly a welcome sight. Immediately below the companionway is a removable entry step which also serves to conceal the ballast tank filling valve. On the starboard side you can see a large plexiglas door to the enclosed head, which has a small fiberglass sink, manual pump, and space for a chemical toilet. Let me assure you that a private toilet area enclosed by four solid walls is a big plus! The rear berth is directly below the cockpit and measures 7' 7" by 6' 3". There is sitting headroom in a decent size area of the berth. Additionally, there is a small storage area under the aft berth.

The total absence of wood gives the interior of the boat a stark and cold feeling. The owner can enhance the appearance of the boat by selective and tasteful use of teak in the interior. If done

Photo 1-7. Inside the cabin of a MacGregor 26X, the dinette table
can be lowered to convert to a double berth

carefully with attention to detail (rounding, joints, etc.) the interior
can be made to look truly cozy and inviting.

The cockpit is over six-feet long and provides maximum seating for six people and comfortable seating for four. In the rear of the
cockpit is the pedestal for the wheel steering that is standard on the
MacGregor 26X. At the very aft end of the cockpit, behind the
pedestal, is the steering seat which hinges up and creates a walk-
through transom for easy boarding. This is particularly important
for smaller people because this boat has a good size freeboard.

One thing I really like about the MacGregor 26X is that it has
solid, positive foam flotation material installed high in the boat.
What this means is that the boat will remain afloat if it is damaged.
Even when filled with water, the boat will return to an upright

position with its deck exposed. This feature greatly enhances the safety of the boat and is a positive consideration for families with small children.

With the new 26X MacGregor has raised the quality of construction of its boats. A lot of my friends are still put off by the low price, saying, "you get what you pay for." I am absolutely convinced that the old adage does not apply in this case. With the MacGregor 26X you get an awful lot of boat with plenty of living space for your money. The water ballast system makes it really easy to tow. It performs well and is easy to sail when properly rigged and equipped. Finally, with a little thought and additional money, it can be nicely personalized to fit your needs and taste. I strongly recommend this boat.

The Hunter 240

The Hunter 240 is only one of many sailboat models manufactured by the Hunter Marine Corporation of Alachua, Florida. It is the only Hunter model that meets both the weight and the width requirements listed earlier, and that can be outfitted to permit you to sail big. While the Hunter 26 is a water ballasted sailboat that is said to be trailerable, due to its beam (almost nine feet) a permit would be required in any state in the country. Additionally, with its ballast tank full the Hunter 26 weighs 5000 pounds, and that is a little too much weight to haul out of the water with the typical automobile or van sold in America. Here are the basic numbers:

PRINCIPAL SPECIFICATIONS

Length Overall (LOA)	24' 1"
Waterline Length (LWL)	22' 1"
Beam	8' 3"
Sail Area (100% triangles)	242 sq. ft.
Mast Height (above waterline)	32' 6"
Displacement (dry)	2300 lbs.
Water Ballast	1300 lbs.
Draft, board up	1' 6"

Photo 1-8. The Hunter 240

board down	5' 6"
Fresh-water Capacity	6.5 gal.

What You Get. The Hunter 240 is delivered to the buyer equipped with a Cruise Pac consisting of a lengthy list of equipment that is optional on comparable sailboats. In other words, with the Hunter 240 you get a whole lot more than just a basic boat. Here's the standard Hunter 240:

Standard Boat and Equipment: Hunter 240

1. The boat with molded-in accent stripe and nonskid surfaces on the deck
2. Anchor well
3. Stainless steel bow pulpit, stern railings, lifelines, and stainless swim ladder

4. Outboard engine bracket built-in
5. Kick-up rudder
6. Pop-top cabin
7. Walk-through transom
8. Mainsail with full battens and 110% genoa
9. Anodized aluminum mast and boom with internal halyards
10. Jiffy reefing
11. Galley with fiberglass sink, manual pump, five-gallon fresh-water capacity, and one-burner stove
12. Portable ice chest
13. Portable toilet with privacy curtain
14. Dinette table for use in the cabin or cockpit
15. Running lights
16. Interior lights
17. Electrical panel
18. Anchor and line
19. Life jackets
20. Hand held flares
21. Throwable device (PFD)
22. Fire extinguisher
23. U.S. Sailing's *Keel Boat Manual*
24. Positive flotation

Like the MacGregor 26X, the Hunter 240 has a flush deck design. It is less traditional in appearance than the Catalina 22markII, but more so than the MacGregor 26X. The molded-in accent stripe ends at the transom in a sort of cute squibble which, in my opinion, detracts from the boat's overall appearance. I've been on this boat several times and I always find that when sitting in the cockpit it is not easy to see forward over the cabin top. For people shorter than I am, visibility might be truly hampered. I would suggest that you check this out for yourself. Let's look inside the Hunter 240.

Photo 1-9 shows the cabin looking forward through the companionway hatch. Although a little bright, it is pleasing to the eyes. There are settees to port and starboard, with the starboard settee being the longest. The portable ice chest is located under the

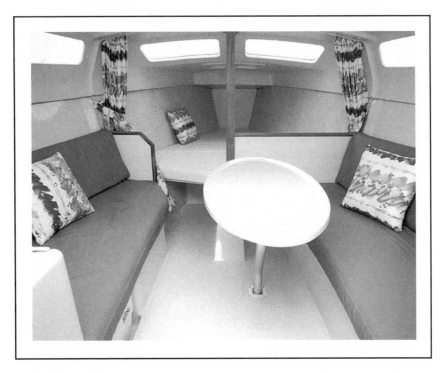

Photo 1-9. Inside the cabin of a Hunter 240, looking forward through the companionway hatch

aft end of the port settee adjacent to the galley. In the middle of the cabin is a molded fiberglass dinette table which is mounted on an aluminum pedestal that inserts into the cabin sole. There is a similar insert for the dinette table in the cockpit which allows for dining by moonlight. I like that a lot. Forward of the port and starboard bulkheads there is a good size V-berth. The Hunter 240 has a chemical toilet arrangement similar to the one on the Catalina 22markII—filler boards and all. When nature calls, you must go through a maneuver similar to the one outlined earlier for the Catalina. If you have a guest you are trying to impress on board, you should probably discuss the necessary maneuvers before bedding down in the V-berth. Luckily, the privacy curtains are standard equipment. While there is not a lot of wood in this cabin, the mast-step compression pole is hidden and the wooden accents on the bulkheads are a nice touch.

At the aft end of the cabin is a good size double berth located under the cockpit. The galley area contains a small, fold-down preparation platform on the right side. There is storage in the galley, as well as under every berth in the cabin.

The cockpit is large and comfortable for a boat this size. It is T-shaped and has a small bridgedeck. The walk-through transom is a nice feature, and for those with children who enjoy swimming, the standard swim ladder is a big plus. I wish the tiller were made from wood instead of aluminum.

Like the MacGregor 26X, the Hunter 240 has positive flotation built in. I am also partial to the added headroom provided by the hinged seahood (pop-top). Like the Catalina 22markII, the Hunter 240 is well constructed, with noticeable attention to detail. It's a good looking boat. It is nice and responsive under sail, it comes very well equipped, and will keep its value. I recommend that you give this boat serious consideration.

The Catalina 250

In response to the water ballast sailboats introduced first by Mac-Gregor and subsequently by Hunter, Catalina Yachts introduced its own version of a trailerable, water ballasted sailboat in 1995. As an avid trailer-sailor, and as one who has become convinced of the practical utility of the concept of water ballast, I was quite interested in the Catalina 250. I have owned and sailed on a lot of Catalina sailboats and have always been impressed with the quality of their construction and their user friendly nature. I was, therefore, ready to examine the new Catalina 250. Let's take a look at the vital statistics:

PRINCIPAL SPECIFICATIONS
Length Overall (LOA)	25' 0"
Waterline Length (LWL)	21' 3"

Photo 1-10. The Catalina 250

Beam	8' 6"
Sail Area	268 sq. ft.
Displacement (dry)	2400 lbs.
Water Ballast	1200 lbs.
Draft, board up	1' 8"
Draft, board down	5' 9"
Fresh-water capacity	5 gal.
Fuel Locker	6 gal.

What You Get. As is traditional with Catalina Yachts, the standard Catalina 250 is delivered well equipped. This is a very attractive sailboat when viewed in profile. When you watch the boat underway or just admire its graceful sheer at anchor, the Catalina 250 gives the impression of being a properly found small yacht. Here is the basic boat as delivered from Catalina Yachts.

Standard Boat and Equipment: Catalina 250

1. The boat with molded-in sheer stripe, boot-top, and non-skid surfaces on the deck
2. Bow pulpit, stern pulpit, lifelines, and swim ladder
3. Molded-in toerail on foredeck and cabin top
4. Anodized aluminum mast and boom with internal halyards led to cockpit
5. Mainsail with full battens and 110% genoa
6. Running lights
7. Anchor light on masthead and steaming light on mast
8. Galley with stainless sink, one-burner stove with sea rail, manual water pump, and five-gallon fresh-water container
9. Removable ice chest
10. Teak interior trim
11. Removable cabin table for mounting in cockpit
12. Molded-in anchor and fuel lockers
13. Opening forward hatch
14. Walk-through transom
15. Jiffy reefing for mainsail
16. Genoa tracks and blocks on adjustable cars
17. Boom vang
18. Mast carrier
19. Manual bilge pump with through-deck handle
20. Outboard motor bracket
21. Pop-top cabin
22. Private enclosed head compartment with opening port
23. Portable marine toilet and paper holder
24. Built-in hanging locker/storage compartment
25. Sink and vanity in head with fresh-water pump
26. 12-volt D.C. electrical system with control panel and marine battery
27. Interior lights
28. Wooden tiller

Let's examine the accommodations and amenities of the Catalina 250.

Photo 1-11 shows the cabin looking forward from just aft of the galley area. The cabin is bright and airy while at the same time nicely softened by the use of varnished teak. A large U-shaped settee

Photo 1-11. Inside the cabin of a Catalina 250 looking forward from aft of the galley area

surrounds the main cabin and the dinette table is attached to the mast-step compression pole. Just beneath the large white dining table you can see the smaller table that is also fixed amidships. The larger table can be removed from the compression pole and stored away when not in use, or, alternatively, the table can be mounted in the cockpit. The hardware for cockpit mounting is built-in. Immediately behind the U-shaped settee is the forward V-berth which is easily prepared for sleeping. An opening forward hatch provides additional ventilation in the cabin, and the large recessed windows let in lots of light. There is also built-in interior lighting that is quite good for a boat this size.

The aft end of the cabin is illustrated in Photo 1-12, which provides a view looking back from the V-berth area. The first thing you see is the enclosed head compartment which has a vanity, a

Photo 1-12. Inside the cabin of a Catalina 250 looking aft from the V-berth area

sink, and a hanging locker. An opening port in this enclosed area adds a thoughtful touch. As with the MacGregor 26X, the enclosed head is a welcome and luxurious addition for weekending or extended cruising. On the starboard side, directly across from the enclosed head, is the galley. Here you will find a stainless sink, a one-burner stove with sea rail, fresh-water storage and a manual fresh-water pump. This galley comes with a good size surface to the right of the stove which can be used for food preparation and a little shelf area for storing glasses and other small items. A removable ice chest is stored conveniently beneath the counter. There is good galley storage for a boat this size. Something I also like about this galley is the plexiglas fiddle that wraps around the whole area to prevent things from crashing to the cabin sole.

Photo 1-12 also shows the three-step ladder leading from the cockpit into the main cabin. The bottom step is created by the housing for the ballast tank filler valve. Further aft, under the cockpit, is the large double berth. Of the three water ballasted boats we have talked about, this aft berth is the easiest to enter and to leave.

The cockpit is of adequate size and has well-contoured coamings for decent back support. There are two lockers and a small bridgedeck and, as I mentioned earlier, the cabin table can be brought out and set up for outdoor dining. The standard stainless swim ladder is great for reboarding the boat after a refreshing dip, and for those with children on board, the stern pulpit gives an added sense of security. While the MacGregor 26X is delivered with wheel steering, the standard Catalina 250 has a tiller. You can order wheel steering if you want it, but it is optional and expensive.

This is a good-looking sailboat with lots of room and amenities. In order to increase the space the beam would need to be expanded which in turn would add a lot more weight. That's what Hunter did with its 26-footer and, as a result, it would take a very strong vehicle to tow it. With the 250, I believe that Catalina has just about optimized the balance between interior volume and towing weight. Like other Catalinas, this is a well-built boat that sails nicely. It is comfortable and practically laid-out for weekending or longer cruises. This boat will be sought after and it will retain its value. I give this trailerable sailboat very high marks.

A COMPARISON: STANDARD AND OPTIONAL EQUIPMENT

Now that we have talked about the four most popular trailerable sailboats sold in this country, we are faced with the most daunting question of all: How do you decide which boat to buy? More than likely the most decisive factors are going to be your personal taste, the "feel" you get when you climb aboard, and the pleasure you derive from sailing on each boat.

Let me try to help you along. As a first step you can compare the equipment available for each boat. Table 1 lists equipment that is standard or optional on the production models of the four trailerable sailboats we have discussed. There are 37 items listed in the table, and you can draw your own conclusions. Permit me, however, to say the obvious—a signal horn doesn't cost as much as a deck light, and a stove isn't nearly as expensive as recessed genoa tracks and cars. Also, a boat delivered with a custom-made trailer is a boat delivered with a very costly item, and a trailer fitted to properly support the boat will help to prolong your new boat's life.

Finally, as I mentioned earlier, don't forget the other eight sailboats on the list—they are all fine trailerables and deserve your attention as well.

TABLE 1

	Catalina 22markII	MacGregor 26X	Hunter 240	Catalina 250
Mainsail, w/reef-points	S	S	S	S
Jib sail, w/sheets	S	S	S	S
Pop-top cabin	S	NA	S	S
Anchor locker	S	S	S	S
Electrical system,w/panel	S	S	S	S
Cabin lights	S	S	S	S
Running lights	S	S	S	S
Marine battery	S	S	S	S
Steaming light on mast	O	S	O	S
Anodized aluminum mast and boom	S	S	S	S
Halyards internal in mast	S	NA	S	S
Galley w/sink and water system	O	S	S	S
Stove	O	O	S	S
Genoa tracks w/cars	S	NA	O	S

Anchor light on masthead	O	NA	O	S
Deck lights on mast	O	NA	NA	O
Bow pulpit	S	S	S	S
Sternrail (pulpit)	S	S	S	S
Primary winches (2)	S	S	S	S
Fuel tank compartment	S	S	S	S
Lifelines and stanchions	O	S	S	S
Fabric cushions	S	S	S	S
Dinette table	NA	S	S	S
Cockpit table	NA	NA	S	S
Chemical toilet	O	NA	S	S
Enclosed head compartment	NA	S	NA	S
Outboard motor well or bracket	O	S	S	S
Outboard motor	NA	NA	O	NA
Anchor and line	NA	NA	S	NA
Life jackets	NA	NA	S	NA
Signal horn	NA	NA	S	NA
Throwable device (PFD)	NA	NA	S	NA
Manual bilge pump	O	NA	S	S
Kick-up rudder	O	S	S	O
Interior carpet	O	S	O	O
Boom vang	O	O	S	S
Custom trailer	O	S	S	O

S = Standard
O = Optional
NA = Not available from the manufacturer

Table 2 presents another list of equipment, standard on some boats and optional on others, and the associated costs. All prices are approximate. We will talk about several of the items in this table in Chapter 6, "The Necessities" and in Chapter 7, "The Amenities."

TABLE 2

1. Trailer ($1,500 - $2,000)
2. Cabin curtains ($75)
3. Chemical toilet ($150)

4. Stove ($150 - $350)
5. Boom vang ($175)
6. Outboard motor bracket ($200)
7. Aft-led halyard kit and winches ($500)
8. Cockpit cushions ($250-$300)
9. Mainsail cover ($200)
10. Tiller cover ($50)
11. Shore power connection ($225)
12. Pop-top cover ($200)
13. Outboard motor ($3,000 - $4,000)
14. 5-gallon gas tank and bulb ($35)
15. Jib downhaul ($35)
16. Roller furling (Jib) ($450)
17. Stern-mounted fold-down swim ladder ($250)
18. Bimini ($450)
19. VHF radio and antenna ($300)
20. Compass and compass cover ($200)
21. Depth sounder ($300)
22. Masthead fly ($30)
23. Interior carpet ($100)

If you total the cost of the items in Table 2 you get a figure of between $8,000 to 10,000. There are even more items you will need to have but don't panic! Remember Cardwell's First Law of Sailing Big—*it is easier to sail big in a small sailboat than it is to sail small in a big sailboat.* You can either spend about $20,000 to buy a trailerable boat and make it sail big, or you can spend $95,000-$110,000 buying and properly equipping a 35-foot sailboat.

➢ SUMMARY ≺

You know your own personal situation and circumstances. If your profession, your family, and other factors in your life will permit you to sail month-long cruises in deep blue water, by all means consider a boat in the 30- to 45-foot range. Remember that you may have to leave it at a facility with deep water, perhaps hours away. If, on the other hand, your sailing will be limited to weekends, or short cruises in nearby waters, consider sailing big on a trailerable sailboat. You can keep the boat in your own backyard, or at a local lakeside storage lot or marina. It's easy to see which boat will get the most regular and frequent use, and provide the most pleasure at a reasonable cost.

2
Sails and Motors

The forces at work are the same for any size sail-boat, be they eight or 80 feet in length.

E.S. MALONEY, Chapman Piloting

➢ SAILS ≺

Aside from the boat itself, the most important, and probably the most expensive items to come with the sailboat are the sails. The sails, of course, are the primary source of power for a sailboat, and sail adjustment, or what most sailors call "trim," is the single most important thing we do in determining how efficiently our sailboat moves through the water. It makes good sense, therefore, to know the basic sail types, as well as when to use or "fly" them.

There are a host of different sails you can use on your trailer-able sailboat, but because of the location and purpose of most of the sailing done by the owners of these boats, we will only discuss four of them, the main, the jib, the genoa, and the spinnaker.

I need to point out that the technology involved in producing sails has become quite sophisticated, with sails being designed, cut, and sewn with the assistance of computers. I mention this to let you know that I don't intend to get into a highly technical dis-cussion about sail design, fabrication, and manufacturing; rather, my goal is simply to acquaint you with the most common sails used on trailerable sailboats, identify the basic parts of the sails, and provide a few hints on maintenance and care that will con-tribute to longer life for your sails. Because most trailerable sail-boats are delivered with the mainsail and jib, let's talk about them first.

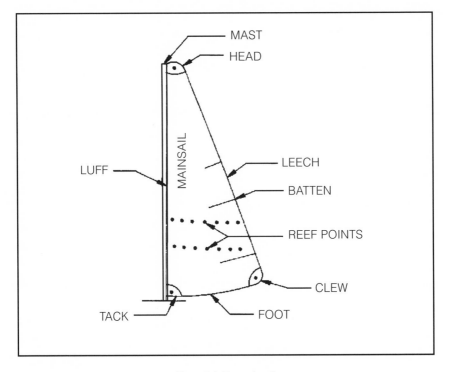

Figure 2-1. The mainsail

The Mainsail

Of the four basic sail types, the *main* is the most basic. It is the primary engine of the sailboat. The main is a large triangular sail (Figure 2-1) which attaches to the rear of the mast at the *luff,* and to the boom at the *foot.* In general, the sail is inserted into channels in the mast and boom, being held in place by slides or, in some cases, *boltropes.*

The trailing edge of the sail is called the *leech.* To help the sail hold its shape, as well as the breeze, stiffeners called *battens* are inserted into pockets sewn into the leech of the sail. There are eyelets located at the *head, tack,* and *clew* of the sail. The main halyard is attached to the head, the outhaul is attached to the clew, and the tack is secured above the gooseneck fitting at the junction of the mast and the boom. The mainsail will also have eyelets sewn at up to three different levels across the width of the sail for reducing sail area ("reefing") when the wind picks up.

Because the main is the principal sail on a trailerable sail-boat, it is used in a wide variety of wind conditions, and is subject to a lot of stress and strain. It needs, therefore, to be well cared for in order to maintain its strength and shape. It's not difficult to do. Here are a few simple suggestions.

First, check the stitching in the sail frequently and repair any sewn areas that have broken or unraveling stitching. A good place to begin an inspection of the sail is any area where it rubs against spreaders, shrouds, lifelines, or lifeline stanchions.

Second, keep the sail clean by occasionally hosing it off with fresh water and allowing it to dry. If you sail in salt water it is par-ticularly important to wash the sail because salt granules will adhere to the sail and attract moisture when it is stored. Be absolutely sure the sail is completely dry before storing, or you will find yourself engaged in a hopeless battle with mold and mildew.

Third, don't wrap the mainsail around the boom and leave it exposed to the damaging effects of the sun and other elements. Your best bet is to buy a mainsail cover to protect it from the weakening effects of prolonged exposure.

Despite heavy use, if you take good care of your mainsail it should last for a long time.

The Jib

The jib is a headsail which attaches to the stemhead fitting at the tack, and then is hooked to and run up the headstay. As you can see from Figure 2-2, the jib usually has less square footage of sail area than the main.

The suggestions I made about maintaining the mainsail also apply to the jib, and all other sails you have on the boat. You can buy jib storage bags that allow you to protect the sail while leaving it attached to the forestay. A jib is not really much trouble to put on or take off, so I prefer to take it down when I'm finished sailing and

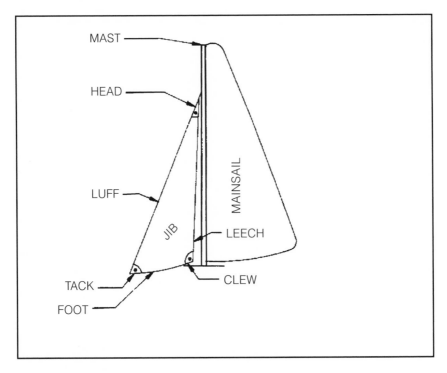

Figure 2-2. The jib

store it inside the cabin in a standard sailbag. It isn't much bigger than a bedsheet, and doesn't take up much room down below.

Before we move on to talk about the genoa and spinnaker, let me offer you some advice about buying additional sails. Most trailerable sailboats are delivered with a mainsail and a standard working jib, and I think you should initially acquaint yourself with the boat using only those two sails. In my opinion, it would be a mistake to rush out and buy some expensive new sails that you may use only infrequently, or never. Not only are genoas and spinnakers expensive, they are much larger sails and require more effort to handle, not to mention more experience to use properly. I advise you to master the main and the jib, for at least one season, before moving on to larger, more specialized sails. Your sailing will probably be easier, and will certainly be less complicated.

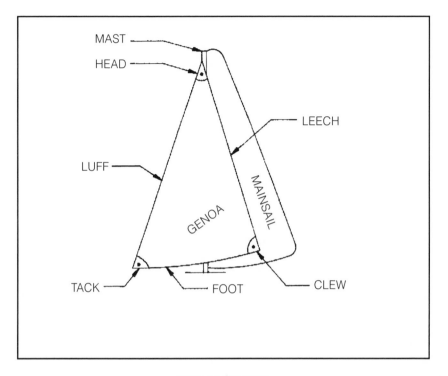

Figure 2-3. The genoa

The Genoa

A genoa is simply a jib that overlaps the mast and part of the main-sail (Figure 2-3). It has more sail area than the working jib, and is most helpful in lighter air. However, it needs to come down and be replaced by a jib when the wind increases in velocity. A word of caution—handling a flapping genoa in a heavy wind is much more difficult than working with a jib.

The Spinnaker

A spinnaker is a three-cornered headsail constructed of very light material, such as rip-stop nylon. Flown forward of the mast and in place of—or sometimes along with—the jib or genoa, a spinnaker

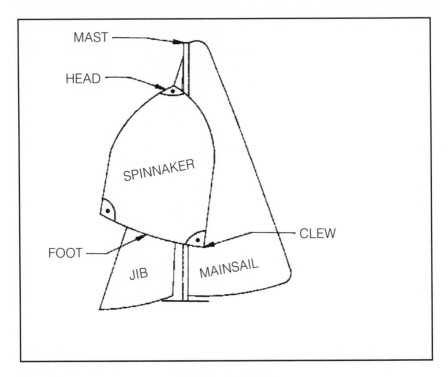

Figure 2-4. The spinnaker

is designed primarily to enhance the downwind performance of the boat (Figure 2-4). The luff on a spinnaker is the windward edge of the sail, and the leech is the leeward edge.

From my point of view the spinnaker is the most difficult of the four sails to hoist and lower, and therefore, it requires the most effort and skill to use. If you don't plan to race your trailerable sailboat, I wouldn't recommend that you invest in a spinnaker.

Summary

I would bet that the majority of people don't know a whole lot about how the motor in their car is put together or, for that matter, the aerodynamic principles involved in the design of the car. Most of us don't worry too much about those things and are content to do the routine maintenance on our car and expect it to keep running like it is supposed to run. The same, I might add, is true of sails.

I can't design sails for maximum aerodynamic efficiency, or put them together in a way that enhances their durability in the face of stress and strain. Just as I can drive my car, however, I can trim the sails and make the boat go. I can also care for my sails and prolong their useful life. You don't have to be a professional sailmaker to enjoy sailing. Just take care of your sails, know which ones to use when, and trim them properly. Enjoy!

➣ MOTORS ≺

People go sailing for a lot of different reasons. We go in search of freedom, adventure, and solitude; to commune with nature, and to develop self-reliance. In doing all of these things, sailors take great pride in the fact that our sport is one which lives in harmony with the elements of nature. In addition to all of the above reasons, many of us are attracted to the quiet elegance and beauty of sailing. Is sailing a sport that is always quietly beautiful and environmentally sensitive? Not quite.

Just take a look at any busy marina at the height of the season. How in the world are those boats going to sail away from such crowded slips? In particular, how are the sailboats that are tied up stern-out going to sail away? You guessed it, they're not. What they are going to do is crank their motors, pollute the water, shatter the quiet, and motor out of the marina into an open area where they can hoist their sails. Because motors pollute the water and give off noxious odors, most sailors have a sort of "love-hate" relationship with them. Unfortunately, motors are useful to have. In addition to helping us exit and reenter a crowded marina or mooring area, they are great to have on those very rare occasions when the wind completely disappears. Starting your motor will give you real pleasure on a humid, 95-degree, sun-drenched day when the breeze decides to take a vacation.

And what about those days when the wind really picks up, the swells begin to grow in size, the spray begins to fly, and crashing through the elements under sail really becomes a bone-shattering, nerve-rattling experience? Well, it is a comfort to be able to lower your sails, start the motor, and make decent headway under such conditions. It is also nice to be able to drop your sails and motor into some out-of-the-way slough or cove. In spite of the fact that they are noisy and stinky, a 22- to 26-foot trailerable sailboat needs a motor!

A trailerable sailboat needs an outboard motor of between five and ten horsepower, with a sufficiently long shaft to keep the prop immersed when the motor is running. Let's look briefly at what you need in the way of an outboard motor.

Horsepower

While an outboard motor with five horsepower will move any of the popular 22- to 26-foot trailerable sailboats along fairly nicely at full power, I do recommend a 10-hp. motor. With a 10-hp. outboard you can get the same speed while running the motor at about half-throttle. If you run the 10-hp. motor at full speed, a five-hp. outboard cannot keep up. This can make a difference.

One hellishly hot summer day I had been sailing on the Intracoastal Waterway, along with three other boats, when the breeze completely vanished. Because we were about seven miles from our destination, we decided to motor the four miles back to the marina. Although the other three boats had 10-hp. motors, I only had a five. You can guess the rest. My colleagues took off like shots and left me to puttering back home. When I did finally arrive, my fellow boaters hooted and cheered from their cockpits.

More horsepower means more expense, but convenience and extra power when needed are worth something. In addition, I think it would be unseemly to outfit your trailerable sailboat to sail "big" in every way, and then equip it with an underpowered outboard motor. The difference in size between a five- and 10-hp. outboard is not significant, so that shouldn't be a consideration.

Regardless of the power of the motor you install, you need to make certain that it has forward, neutral, and reverse gears. In addition, you should plan to have a gas tank external to the motor for those occasions when you may be required to power for an extended period of time. Running out of fuel a long way from landfall is no joy. Finally, an electric starter would be very nice, and you are more likely to find one on a 10-hp. outboard than on a five-hp. motor.

Length of the Shaft

If your trailerable sailboat requires that you mount an outboard motor bracket on the transom, it will be important for you to own a motor with a long shaft, so that the prop won't come out of the water as your boat bobs up and down on the swells. That's not good for the motor, or for making reasonable headway in even moderate seas.

Summary

Don't automatically buy an outboard motor from your sailboat dealer. Instead, shop around. Lots of businesses sell outboard motors, and you may be able to make a deal that is much better than what your sailboat dealer can offer.

I also recommend that you visit the nearest marina and talk with the owners about the outboard motors they have on their sailboats. Ask them about ease of starting, how it moves the boat, and fuel efficiency. More importantly, ask them if they would buy the same motor again. If they say no, ask what they would buy, and why. It sure helps to learn from the mistakes of other people instead of making your own.

Although outboard motors and the attendant noise, pollution, and odor are not wholly compatible with the grace and beauty of sailboats, they are useful labor-saving and safety devices you need on your boat.

3
Topsides

Comfort is not a measureable quality, mainly because it means different things to different people. It also changes according to the weather, the time of year, the size of the boat, the distance from land, the prevalence of seasickness, and the state of the drinks locker.

IAN NICOLSON, Comfort in the Cruising Yacht

➤ INTRODUCTION ◄

In considering the various layouts and arrangements of a trailerable sailboat, bear in mind that a number of factors contribute to the boat's ability to help you sail big. When viewed by a nonsailor from the dock, the occupants of a passing sailboat appear to be simply relaxing, enjoying the breeze, and perhaps sipping something cool. While the observation may be correct, the fact that the sailors are relaxed is not an accident. A lot of thought, planning, and a significant amount of money make the appearance possible. In this chapter we will consider some of the factors that contribute to making the owner of a trailerable sailboat as relaxed as the skipper of a 35- to 40-foot boat.

➤ DECK LAYOUT ◄

Deck layout refers to everything above the gunwales, but mostly to the surface of the deck itself. Essentially, there are two configurations we can talk about—a deck with a traditional trunk cabin (Catalina 22 or Hunter 23), or one with a flush deck design

(MacGregor 26). There are several things to consider here, including which look appeals to you the most. The trunk cabin gives a more traditional look, while the flush deck configuration provides a more sleek and modern look. As we will soon discover, however, you may have to settle for a boat with a deck layout you prefer the least in order to acquire other features which will make your sailing more enjoyable.

In addition to offering a more traditional look, the trunk cabin deck creates a little room to walk between the sides of the cabin and the gunwales of the boat. There are those who would argue that even a small walking space is important when one has to go forward to loosen a sheet, a halyard, or to accomplish some other task. Still, for someone like me, with size 12 feet, there is not a lot of room provided in which to be sure-footed. Add lifeline stanchions to the boat and the available walking surface gets even smaller and, at times, hazardous. Before I give the impression that such an area is useless, let me point out that being able to grab hold of a cabintop handrail when walking in this area is a definite plus, particularly when the boat has a substantial heel to it.

On the flush deck design the only place to walk when going forward is on the cabintop itself. There are no handrails to grab when you are up there and the boat heels. About the only thing one can do under such circumstances is to grab the shrouds or the mast.

Most boats with either the traditional trunk cabin or the flush deck cabin do provide a hatch in the foredeck area through which one can gain access to that part of the boat, thus reducing the need to walk on slippery surfaces in the first place.

The bottom line here is appeal and, to an important extent, safety. Personally, the trunk cabin design appeals to me the most, but the safety factor of the walking area is offset by the fact that I am insecure in such a restricted amount of space. I choose the flush deck design.

➤ BOW PULPITS AND STERNRAILS ≺

These two attachments are items I consider necessities. Bow pulpits give you a sense of security in the foredeck area. They will keep you from falling over the bow of the boat, and they will give you something to grab onto if you should slip or fall nearby. Bow pulpits need to be of welded construction, and not of sections held together by nuts and bolts or pop rivets. When attached, bow pulpits need to be through-bolted, not held in place by self-tapping screws.

Sternrails are also very important. Designed primarily to keep you on the boat when sitting in the rear of the cockpit, sternrails also serve other functions. They allow you to hand an "O" ring or some other man-overboard device from the rail, to mount a grill for outdoor cooking, to attach flag poles, or to hang a variety of other things such as a VHF radio antenna, drink holders, etc.

➤ LIFELINES ≺

In theory lifelines are designed to help keep you on the boat. Practically, however, the lifelines one usually finds on boats from 22- to 26-feet and on bigger boats, for that matter, will serve their theoretical purpose only if you are a young child or a very small adult. If you are a normal-size adult, these accessories will usually rise to about knee level. If you are six feet or more, they will strike you slightly below the knees, in just the right place to trip you up. On sailboats of the size we are talking about, these things are mostly cosmetic, although they do help make a boat look "finished." Lifelines allow the small-boat sailor to hang fenders (bumpers) or to dry wet towels or clothing in the breeze.

➤ HATCHES ≺

Hatches are lids on the exterior of the boat that lead to the interior cabin area, to anchor lockers, or to storage areas in the cockpit. On the boats we are concerned with there are usually two hatches giving access to the cabin—the companionway hatch and the foredeck hatch. The companionway hatch slides on cabintop runners in such a manner that when it is closed it completely covers the companionway. When opened it is pushed forward toward the mast, opening the cabin to additional light and air. The foredeck hatch is located on the forward portion of the cabin or on the foredeck, immediately in front of the cabin. These hatches are designed to increase light and airflow through the cabin when open. As has been mentioned earlier, foredeck hatches can be used to gain access to the foredeck area when necessary.

Hatches need to fit neatly with the surrounding part of the boat and should have adequately deep and properly contoured drainways to keep them from leaking. It is no fun to walk on a wet interior carpet or to try to sleep on a V-berth that is soaked from rain or spray that found its way into the boat. All hatches that raise and lower should be attached with hinges that are through-bolted and not mounted with self-tapping screws. Regardless of the material they are made of, hatches should be sturdy enough for an adult to walk or sit on. Foredeck hatches need to have a hold-open device attached so you can open them as much or as little as you want.

➤ SAIL CONTROL LINES TO COCKPIT ≺

If you are the least bit serious about sailing big on a trailerable sailboat, an arrangement for leading halyards and other lines back to the cockpit is absolutely essential.

Imagine, if you will, what it would be like to be alone on the boat without such a system. Suppose the breeze is blowing about

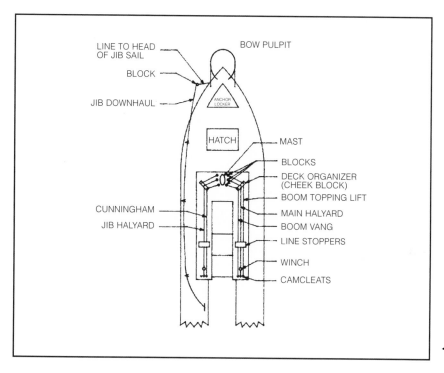

Figure 3-1. Aft-led halyard system: top view

15 knots. You let go of the tiller and climb onto the cabintop to raise the sails. Of course, you uncleat the main and jib sheets to permit the sails to luff in the breeze while you are up there, and the tiller is unattended. What happens, however, if the breeze shifts to the other side, one of the sheets gets snagged, and a sail fills while you are still up there all alone? What do you do when the boat starts to sail away? Well, the point is that you usually don't have to put up with such problems if you have a system for leading your halyards and other lines back aft to the cockpit. Let's look at Figure 3-1, which is an overhead view of one possible arrangement.

We begin installing the system by locating blocks (pulleys) at the base of the mast. If your boat doesn't have a provision for doing so, you may have to purchase a mast-step plate or have the blocks bolted to the cabin roof. In the example in Figure 3-1, I have installed six blocks to handle the main and jib halyards, a boom topping lift, the boom vang, and a cunningham. As you can see, one block is vacant for future additions. At about the curvature of the cabintop, I have installed a deck organizer with three turning blocks angled to enable the halyards to turn the corner and head back toward the cockpit. The lines are then led aft to and through a line stopper which accommodates three lines. The line for the boom vang is passed through the line stopper and back to a cam cleat mounted on the end of the cabintop. The boom topping lift and main halyard are routed in the same manner, except the halyard is led to a winch first, and then to the cam cleat. The halyard winch makes it easier to hoist the mainsail. The cunningham and jib halyard are routed in a similar manner on the port side.

With this arrangement all you need to do is remove the mainsail retaining cords, raise the sails from the cockpit, and sail away. Upon returning, the procedure is reversed, you uncleat the halyards and let the sails drop. Even if you must assist the mainsail by pulling on it from the cockpit, it is still a whole lot easier than climbing up on the cabintop to drop the sail.

The standard working jib is a smaller and lighter sail than the main and sometimes it really hesitates to drop to the deck when the jib halyard is uncleated. The force of gravity has less effect on this sail and the breeze has a tendency to keep it up the headstay, flapping in the wind. To avoid having to leave the cockpit and getting white knuckles trying to take down the jib, you can install a downhaul device that will enable you to bring the jib to the deck from the cockpit.

➤ JIB DOWNHAULS ◄

They are quite simple and inexpensive to install. Even though they are not complicated, downhaul rigs will contribute significantly to your sailing comfort. The system requires (1) a small block with a

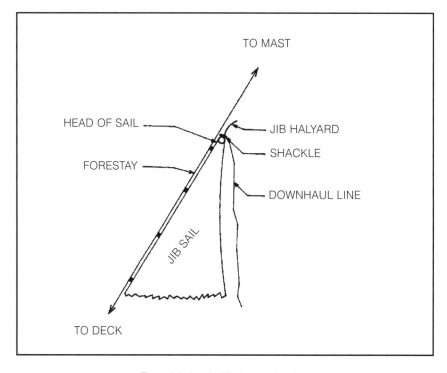

Figure 3-2. A typical jib downhaul system

sheave that will handle a 1/4" line, (2) enough of the line to ride up the headstay with the jib and extend back to the cockpit, and (3) perhaps some fairleads and a small cleat. Figure 3-2 shows how it is set up.

One end of the 1/4" line has a shackle fixed to it and the shackle is fastened around the halyard above the head of the sail. The other end of the line (the "bitter end") is run through a block attached to the bow pulpit and then through the lifeline stanchions. The line is then routed back to the cockpit and can be fixed to a small cleat mounted in a convenient place. If you don't like the idea of routing the downhaul line through the lifeline stanchion bases, you can attach two or three bullseye fairleads on the deck and run it through them to get the line back to the cockpit. When installed, the system is really easy to use. All you do is uncleat the jib halyard from the aft-led system and then pull on the jib downhaul. When you do, the jib will fall politely to the foredeck.

➤ HEADSAIL ROLLER FURLING/REEFING SYSTEMS ◄

A jib downhaul system will make your sailing more comfortable by allowing you to douse the sail from the cockpit. This is really about all it will do. Yet it is nothing to sneer at, particularly when the breeze picks up, the waves begin to build, and the foredeck is wet and slippery. With a jib downhaul you don't have to go forward on a pitching foredeck to lower the jib. However, if you are out there with a genoa flying and the wind increases, you will still have to go forward to remove the genoa and hank on the working jib if you want to reduce sail area. The good news is that unlike downhauls, headsail furling/reefing systems allow you to set and strike the headsail, and to reduce the amount of sail exposed to the breeze, all without leaving the cockpit. Let's take a closer look.

Headsail furling/reefing systems are expensive. For a 22- to 26-foot trailerable sailboat you can expect to spend somewhere between $750 and $1,500. Nevertheless, a lot of trailer-sailors think the convenience and safety of furlers make them well worth the cost. Here's what they allow you to do:

1. Sail off by yourself because the need to replace headsails is reduced;
2. Sail with a large genoa, because you don't have to go forward to reduce the sail area exposed to the wind;
3. Reduce the number of headsails you will need to carry on board; and
4. Fly or douse the sail easily.

I do not want to get into a long description of these systems—you can do more in-depth research and reading about them on your own. Essentially, a headsail furler/reefer is composed of a winding drum which attaches at the stemhead fitting, a long protrusion for housing the headstay, and a swivel that attaches to the protrusion near the top of the headstay. Jib sheets are wound around the inside of the drum at the stemhead fitting, and then run back to the cockpit.

Furling systems operate on the same principle as old fashioned spring-loaded window shades. Just as you pull on the cord to raise the window shade, you pull on the jib sheet to unfurl the sail, and you release it to let it wind up around itself. And like the old fashioned window shades, you can expose as much or as little of its length as you desire.

If you are at all unsure about your ability to install one of the systems, get a professional to do it for you. These systems are too costly to make mistakes with. If you have to hire someone, plan on spending more money.

One final caveat. One of the reasons I don't have a furler/reefer on *Felicity*, my Aquarius 23, is that I am not completely convinced they can withstand the stresses and strains of a real blow. My advice to you is to talk to sailors who have these systems and ask how they feel about them. I would also talk with others who don't have furlers and seek their opinions before making a decision.

➤ SHEET STOPPERS ≺

We have previously mentioned these devices in our discussion of the aft-led halyard system. On trailerable sailboats they are typically used for this purpose only. One piece of advice—they come in sizes to accommodate one, two or three lines and you should buy the size you are most likely to grow into. Doing so will save you a little money and, more importantly, will make your deck look neater than two or three single-sheet stoppers mounted side by side.

➤ DECK LIGHTS ≺

There are a lot of sailors who think that the running lights and a masthead light are all that is needed for a trailerable sailboat. In fact, you can get by fine with just these lights. However, if you want to sail big you need a deck light mounted on the mast. A deck light is fitted to the mast well below the steaming or masthead light, and is designed to illuminate the foredeck area so you can move about safely after the sun goes down. In addition, the more of your boat you can illuminate until the traffic settles down for the evening, the less likely it is that someone will run into you.

➤ THE COCKPIT ≺

Cockpits can be wonderfully pleasant or hellishly awful places in which to spend your time on a sailboat. That's why, over the years, I have been amazed with how much time and money people spend in making the cabins of their sailboats liveable, and how little they spend in making the cockpit as comfortable as possible. They seem to believe that before they are entitled to enjoy a relaxed evening in the cabin, they must somehow earn it by suffering all day in a rude and crude cockpit. I couldn't disagree more. It is a fundamental truth that a sailboat is designed to be sailed from the cockpit. However, it is also true that this space can be used for relaxing and reading, cooking, or entertaining.

On trailerable sailboats, cockpits are usually about six feet long. The major features of this space are the *cockpit seats,* the *sole* (floor), and the *coamings.*

Technically, the coamings are the raised sides of the cockpit; put in everyday terms the coamings are the backrests. The higher they are, the more comfortable the cockpit will be. The coamings should be angled outboard somewhat so that you won't be sitting bolt upright when relaxing in the cockpit, or pitched forward when the boat is heeled over.

About all I can say about the cockpit seats is that they should be wide enough to accommodate a full-sized person's rear-end, and high enough from the sole so your knees are not at your chin when sitting down. The sole of the cockpit should be wide enough for you to move around with relative ease. I have already mentioned that I wear size 12 shoes. My youngest son wears a size 13, and when we both are in the cockpit, a sole with a decent width is a must.

Even if you have small feet you still need a good-size cockpit sole to come to grips with the problem of trash on the floor. Carl Romig has written about the behavior of sailboat lines and trash in the cockpit. "Trash in the cockpit should be properly picked up and put away—not only out of cleanliness and politeness, but to keep it away from the lines. Where empty bags and cans accumulate, a line is sure to come along and start playing with them, lashing itself around them and so forth. Also, paper trash is one of the few things able to jump overboard from inside the cockpit."

I can tell you that Romig has a good understanding of the gregarious nature of sailboat lines. I once had a main sheet that frolicked with an empty beer can, a winch handle, a pair of pliers, and a roll of tape to form a large and complicated ball of line and metal lying in the cockpit sole. I stepped on that ball, turned my ankle, and grabbed the tiller to support myself as I started to fall. Yes, my weight cracked the tiller. Cockpit soles are important.

Assuming that the coamings are adequately high and angled, the seats are wide and high enough, and the sole is of sufficient width, let's look at how the cockpit can be made as "big" as possible, given what we have to work with. Probably the easiest and quickest thing you can do to have an immediate impact on comfort is to add thick cockpit cushions for the seats and the coamings.

A second important addition is a sternrail. Sternrails provide a real sense of security when sailing and are convenient backrests. They also provide a structure to which things can be attached, and from which devices can be hung that will make the cockpit a more desirable place to spend your time. A barbecue grill can be mounted so that it is suspended outside the sternrail and doesn't take up valuable cockpit space. You can also buy drink holders that will attach to the sternrail and sway with the heel of the boat so your drink won't spill. Sternrails are also great places to mount a horseshoe or ring buoy throwable device. The list of things that can be attached to the sternrail goes on and on—cleats, fender holders, umbrellas, etc.

Cockpit cushions are a must. Sternrails help enclose the cockpit, define it as a living space, and make an important contribution to cockpit comfort. If, however, I can make at least one additional recommendation for equipping the cockpit for sailing "big," let me encourage you in the strongest possible way to purchase and install a *bimini top.*

Biminis are to a sailboat cockpit what air-conditioning is to a home in Alabama, Louisiana, or Florida. They represent the final step in transforming the cockpit from a place where one endures the elements to one where one actually enjoys sailing.

A bimini is a large cloth cover made of canvas, vinyl, or some combination of fabrics that is fitted over a metal frame, which is then mounted on the deck or coamings around the cockpit. The basic frame is V-shaped and is bolted to the boat at the bottom of the "V." Fabric hold-downs are then run from the front and rear of the bimini frame, attaching to the lifeline stanchions and the sternrail. When not in use, the bimini folds down over the cabintop. Biminis provide shade from the hot, harmful ultraviolet rays of the sun and make the cockpit a desirable place to relax, read, entertain, cook and eat.

Biminis are not designed to protect the cockpit from rain, particularly when there is an accompanying breeze driving the rain at angles. They do a pretty fair job, however, of controlling the amount of dew in the cockpit, which is a definite plus to bare feet in the early morning hours. If you will think of your cockpit as an extension of the cabin, you will have the general idea. Although biminis are not inexpensive, they are a real bargain if your skin, your sanity, and your enjoyment are worth anything.

Now let's talk about a more mundane and pedestrian matter—mounts or brackets for outboard motors. Of the boats we talked about in Chapter One, the Hunter 240 and the Catalina 250 come with a motor well or bracket molded into the hull. Most do not, and you will usually have to spend some additional money buying a bracket and having it attached. Buy a high-quality bracket, and make certain it will fit the angle of your boat's transom. Also be sure that the bracket is made of stainless steel with an adequately thick mounting board. You should be able to lock the bracket in either an up or down position. Finally, an outboard motor lock isn't a bad idea.

➤ SUMMARY ≺

To summarize our discussion of the deck and cockpit arrangements of trailerable sailboats, let me begin by saying that there is much that could have been mentioned that has been omitted. I have tried to focus on the layouts and systems that relate to sailing "big." Whether we like it or not, people will form opinions about our sailboats, and, therefore about us, based on what they see, and the first thing they will see is the outside of the boat. Happily, there is a good correlation between the appearance and the actuality of sailing big on a trailerable sailboat.

In Chapter 4 we will turn our attention to the living space on a trailerable sailboat—the belowdecks area. Down below the possibilities are as numerous as they are on the topsides. Once again, however, our focus will be on comfort, i.e., "sailing big."

4

Belowdecks

When the anchor is down, the riding light hoisted on the forestay for the night, and the hatch closed against the cool night air, a small yacht's cabin can become the cosiest place in the world.

MAURICE GRIFFITHS, Round the Cabin Table

➢ INTRODUCTION ≺

To begin our discussion of the interior living space on a trailerable sailboat, let's visualize the space inside one of those new vehicles being built by General Motors, Ford, or Chrysler, called "minivan." The space available in a minivan is roughly the same as the space you have to work with in a trailerable sailboat. Our analogy doesn't have to stop with space, because minivans are just like trailerable sailboats in that the vehicle comes equipped ready to "drive away," for a base price. You can purchase the basic minivan and it will surely get you from Point A to Point B. If you desire to go from A to B in real comfort, however, you will have to start adding and paying for a long list of options from power windows to deluxe fabric on the seats. Trailerable sailboats are exactly the same; they come equipped to "sail away" at a base price, but if you want to sail away in comfort, you will have to add and pay for accessories in order to do so.

Three things affect the interior volume of a trailerable sailboat—the beam, the length of the cockpit, and the shape (curvature) of the hull.

In Chapter One we defined the beam of a sailboat as its maximum width. In talking about interior space, however, an important consideration is how quickly the maximum width is lost when moving forward or going aft.

A second factor that affects the living space is the size of the cockpit. Generally speaking, a cockpit can be made larger only by reducing the size of the cabin, and vice versa. My own advice in this area is to sacrifice a little cockpit space to gain some additional room in the cabin. Don't give up too much, however. If you don't have a cockpit large enough to seat four adults in comfort, you can forget entertaining or wiggle room for children in this area. Furthermore, if the cockpit will not accommodate four adults, the probabilities are that you will not be able to stretch out, and relax. You need to be able to do that.

Finally, the shape (curvature) of the hull will have some effect on the available space in the cabin. Sailboats with flatter bottoms usually provide slightly more room side to side than sailboats with more V-shaped underbodies. In trailerable sailboats, however, the difference is usually so small as to be unnoticeable. What is most important is how the boat suits you personally and how well it fits into the plans you have for using the boat. Don't get a boat that you must fit yourself into, get one that fits you. Now let's take a look at some of the factors belowdecks that will affect your ability to sail "big."

➤ VENTILATION ➤

One of the true benefits of a large cockpit on a sailboat is the chance to be out in the fresh air and to enjoy the breeze. The only problem with the cockpit is that unless you are protected from the harsh ultraviolet rays of the sun, the fresh air and the breeze can combine with the sun to do great damage to your exposed skin. Belowdecks, in the cabin, the problem is exactly the opposite. In full sun, fiberglass can get warm quickly, and the heat is transmitted into the cabin in a very short time. What we want to be able to do in the cabin is get as much air flowing through it as possible.

Hatches and pop-tops really help the airflow through the interior of the cabin.

There will be times when you are going to be anchored with the covered pop-top up and there will be absolutely no breeze blowing anywhere—most certainly not in your sailboat cabin. If it's summertime and you are anchored for the evening, you can count on being visited by mosquitoes or the infamous "no-see-ums." Please be sure that all of your hatches have screens.

Okay, there you are. It's a hot summer evening, let's say around 85 degrees, with 87 percent humidity and absolutely no air moving. Every drink you place on any surface immediately leaves a pool of water and every piece of paper you touch sticks to your arm. I mean it is hot and humid. How do you keep cool?

Let's talk about three options. The easiest to install is an electric fan. The secret here is to find an efficient model that minimizes battery drain, yet generates good air flow while oscillating. If I didn't have a Windscoop, which we will talk about next, I would position the fan toward the rear of the cabin and let it blow the air forward. At least I am more comfortable with this arrangement; it may be different for you. There is a wide variety of such fans available from marine supply stores and marine supply catalogs such as West Marine and E&B Discount Marine. I suggest you get a fan designed for marine use. In other words, don't buy one at a discount store.

A second option is the tried-and-true Windscoop. It is relatively inexpensive, requires no electricity, and generally works pretty well. The only catch is that Windscoops do require at least a minimum amount of moving air in order to "do their thing." Fig. 4-1 shows a Windscoop that can be ordered from the West Marine products catalog. The one shown is made from rip-stop nylon, and measures 4 feet wide and 6 feet high. There is a dowel attached to the bottom of the scoop which is inserted inside the hatch to hold it in place. A halyard or topping lift is then attached to a ring on the top of the scoop and it is hoisted upright. Any breeze that is blowing is caught in the scoop just as in a sail, and is directed below into the interior of the cabin. This works really well—so well, in fact, that even the slightest breeze will have a profound cooling effect on the cabin interior.

The third option represents true extravagance. I'm talking about onboard air-conditioning. This is the height of luxury. Small boat air-conditioners come in either a portable or permanent variety. I don't recommend either one, because I would continually worry about the problem of condensation. Also, other than the dramatic initial cost factor, one must consider the fact that these units are appropriate for trailerable sailboats only when the boat is plugged into shore power. I prefer a low-drain electric fan and a Windscoop. With this combination it's possible to stay quite comfortable when anchored on a warm summer evening.

On really rare occasions, all efforts to cool off may fail. If this happens to you, my final suggestion will not fail: Take off your clothes, grab a PFD, and jump right in!

Figure 4-1. A Windscoop

➢ HEADROOM ≺

You may not have given this idea much thought, but it sure helps to be able to sit belowdecks and hold your head up. On most trailerable sailboats in the 22- to 26-foot range, this will not be a problem if you are sitting in or near the center of the boat's cabin. If you are as tall or taller than I am, you know how frustrating it can be to find yourself sitting somewhere with a ceiling so low that you either must slouch down or not raise your head.

On a sailboat with a traditional trunk cabin you will find that the headroom is limited when one occupies the outboard part of the settees. Given the design limitations on trailerable sailboats, there isn't much you can do about this fact. I simply encourage you to sit in several parts of a cabin to make certain you can live with the available headroom.

➢ FOOTROOM ≺

As with the problem of headroom, this is an area that most first-time sailboat buyers usually don't give a lot of thought. You should. I once owned a 19-foot "compact cruiser" with a center-board trunk that intruded into the cabin and split the cabin sole in half. I had to sit slew-footed when I was in the cabin. It was miserable. If you are considering one of the 12 sailboats I listed, or if a manufacturer produces a new model, let me encourage you to check out the footroom in the cabin before you buy.

➢ LIGHTING ≺

With a production model of a trailerable sailboat, you shouldn't have high expectations about lighting in the cabin area. I would say this even if I were talking about sailboats in the 30- to 45-foot range. It's not much of a problem during the daylight hours, particularly if you have a pop-top with your boat, but the pop-top is not much help in increasing light inside the cabin at night. Neither are the manufacturers. What you are going to have to do is shop the marine supply stores and catalogs and purchase some lighting that appeals to you in order to supplement the bare minimum provided by the manufacturer. The available variety of interior lighting is pretty good—from the really nautical to the ultra-modern. You can buy stick-up fluorescent lights or salty-looking lamps fueled by oil. If you like to read at bedtime, a good light in the berth area is essential. You will also be happier if you have good lighting in the galley for working in that area after dark.

One final caveat on minimum lighting requirements is in order. Regardless of whether your toilet is located under a V-berth or has its own enclosed compartment, you will need a light in there at night. I encourage you to think about your own habits and preferences and then buy additional lighting that will enhance your enjoyment and comfort in the late evening hours.

➤ STORAGE ◄

Now for the fun part. Suppose you are going on a four-day cruise with your two children, or your spouse and one child. It will be absolutely no problem to bring everything you need onboard—clothes and food, fuel for cooking, pots, pans, dishes and cups, foul weather gear, ice, games for the children, blankets, towels, etc. However, putting all of this stuff somewhere out of the way will be a problem after you get it on the boat. There is nothing more frustrating or upsetting than to want to sit or lie down and discover that all of the seats and berths are covered with clothes, towels, or bags of food. Furthermore, if you leave this stuff sitting around while you are sailing, it will soon be thrown to the cabin sole when the boat heels or you tack. The answer to this problem is, of course, ample and accessible storage space.

On most trailerable sailboats there is some storage built into the settee berths and the galley. Over time, you can create additional space by personalizing the boat. While visiting other boats, I have found it is truly amazing what people can do to modify the interior of their sailboat cabin to acquire additional storage space.

While having ample storage space is indeed important, equally important is being prepared to use what space you do have to the fullest extent possible. I try to segregate my stuff into different functional areas. For example, I don't mix canned foods with my clothes, or board games with emergency equipment such as flashlights, flares and flare guns. It's also a good idea to carry some plastic bags onboard to keep wet bathing suits and clothes separated from things that you don't want to get wet.

As I mentioned previously, most trailerable sailboats will have storage compartments molded in under most, if not all, of the seats and berths. These offer fairly gracious amounts of storage space. In addition, the boats usually provide some storage space associated with the galley. If you will use what space the manufacturer provides, and do a little creative addition of storage space yourself, you will be able to sail just as big as the guys on the 40-footers. Rest assured, they have a storage problem too.

➤ TOILETS ≺

On trailerable sailboats the bathroom or head is defined as a portable chemical toilet (porta-potti), and it is usually optional on a production model boat. Before you decide that this is an area where you simply can't make up the difference between a small boat and a big boat, let me point out two things. First, the head compartment on a 30-foot sailboat isn't all that terrific. It usually provides you just enough room to bang your elbows and knees into surrounding bulkheads. Second, portable heads are self-contained, and do not discharge their contents overboard and foul the water and marine life. I think that you will agree that it is better to take our waste off of the boat and dispose of it in an environmentally safe manner.

The heads usually come in two parts—a fresh-water tank with about a three-gallon capacity (top), and a holding tank which contains the cleaner/deodorant to treat the waste (bottom). When you return to dock or when all of the fresh water is used, the contents of the holding tank are disposed of in an acceptable receptacle.

In choosing a self-contained head for your boat the best advice I can give you is not to buy a cheap, poorly constructed one. You can settle for a less expensive model, but you will not be pleased that you did. Spring for the "super" model.

After you have returned to shore and disposed of the waste, clean the head. Put a little vinegar water in the holding tank to help keep it smelling fresh. One final piece of advice that you should take very seriously—portable heads should be emptied and cleaned right after returning from a sail, even if you plan to do more sailing in a day or two. This is particularly true in warm weather. Otherwise, when you return to go sailing again the cabin air will be very, very ripe.

➤ THE GALLEY ≺

Although sailboat galleys are not what you would normally associate with the word "kitchen," they do provide all of the equipment and devices necessary for efficient meal preparation. There are, as you might guess, a number of different arrangements for setting-up a galley in a trailerable sailboat. Let's take a look at some of the major features you need to consider when evaluating the galley area.

Sinks

Given the subject of sinks, you would think that there isn't much to talk about, but that really isn't true. Sailboat manufacturers can provide you with sinks that are really functional, or they can provide tiny little bowl-shaped things that are very shallow and will slosh the water out with the slightest heel to the boat. Remember, you will probably find yourself preparing food while sailing, and boats do heel and bob up and down when underway. So the first thing you need to examine is the depth of the sink. Although it is only a guess when looking on dry land, try to satisfy yourself that the sink is deep enough to hold a reasonable amount of water when the boat is heeled. If you can't prepare a meal without fear of getting sloshed with water you will be reluctant to do so when underway, and you will be sailing small.

A second thing to consider is the width and length of the sink. A sink is not very functional if it is too short to hold any utensils or not wide enough to get a small pot down in it for washing. Also, check the finish on the sink. I recommend stainless steel. Some manufacturers provide sinks that are simply molded in as part of the fiberglass hull liner. Sinks made of fiberglass will stain rather easily and are subject to scratching by abrasive cleaners. Finally, and for obvious reasons, there should be some counter space associated with the sink. Don't expect much surface area, but make certain there is some available to put objects down.

Stoves

If you want to talk about a mixed bag of options, this is where to do it. You can get stoves with one or two burners, either flush-mounted or gimballed. You can buy stoves that are fueled by pressurized or nonpressurized alcohol, or butane. There are other combinations as well. More than likely, however, the production model of a trailerable sailboat will come with a provision for a flush-mounted, nonpressurized alcohol stove. While they are okay, I prefer butane because it is instantly hot and cooks in a shorter time.

Examine carefully the location of the stove with one thought in mind: Is there anything immediately above or near the stove that will easily catch fire in case of an accident such as a flare-up when lighting the stove, or because of spilled oil, etc? Look the area over carefully and make certain you can cook safely in that location.

Before I conclude this discussion of stoves, let me elaborate a little on using that grill you have mounted on the sternrail out in the cockpit. It is wonderful for grilling steaks, chicken, or that fresh fish you caught earlier in the day. Once, when I had been sailing with two other boats all day, the three of us anchored at Redfish Point in Florida for the evening. After about an hour at anchor, and just as the sun was dipping behind the horizon, the three boats rafted together. Wayne Townsend, the skipper of one of the boats (a Catalina 22) had been grilling some New York strip steaks. He also had wrapped some vegetables in aluminum foil and thrown them on the coals. After we rafted up, Wayne passed out the steaks and vegetables and we sat there talking and eating one of the most delicious meals I can remember. Don't forget your grill.

Ice Boxes

Ice boxes, or chests, may or may not come as standard equipment on a trailerable sailboat. If it comes standard, there are several things to consider. First, is it large enough to hold any meaningful amount of ice and food or drinks? Remember, you are probably going to have a block of ice in there and there should be adequate room remaining to keep enough food acceptably cool. Second, does it have insulated sides or is it simply a fiberglass container? The chest should have sides that are thick enough to hold some insulation or your ice will not last very long and your food will spoil. Third, the chest should open from the top because cold air falls and you will lose less of that precious commodity if the lid is on top. Finally, it would be great if the chest was sectioned off. If you can keep the block of ice separate from other items, it will last much longer.

If you have an ice chest that is sufficiently large, adequately insulated, sectioned off, and opens from the top, you will be in good shape for sailing big on a short cruise.

Fresh Water

Most trailerable sailboats in our size range will be delivered with a manual fresh water pump and a five-gallon fresh-water tank. These manual pumps work pretty well, requiring somewhere between 45 and 55 strokes to deliver a gallon of water. So you can see that it doesn't take much work to get a glass of fresh water, or enough to make a cup of coffee. One nice thing about manual pumps is that they are uncomplicated mechanisms that are hard to break. If one of these pumps does break, however, it is very easy to repair and the kits for doing so are readily available.

The fresh-water holding tanks can be either rigid or the soft, collapsible variety. The rigid tanks are usually more difficult to clean and maintain, while the collapsible kind can be removed from the boat and filled with fresh water from your home. This last point is a real plus because as you probably know, the fresh water found around most lakesides or coastal marinas has a peculiar taste to it. You may also notice a little plastic taste in your fresh water. If so, a small amount of vinegar water usually helps take the plastic edge out of the taste. If you are going on a cruise that will require more than five gallons of fresh water, try carrying some of those one-gallon jugs of fresh water onboard to replenish your supply. It sure tastes better than marina water.

➢ DINING AREA ➢

Okay, you have used your galley area to prepare an evening's repast and you are ready to dine. The pop-top is raised, the cover installed, the Windscoop is up, and there is a gentle breeze moving through the cabin. The white wine has been chilled in the ice chest. You uncork the wine and find a great stereo station with some soft and gentle music. It's time to sit down and enjoy your dinner.

If this rather pleasant scene is to continue, you will need a comfortable place to set the silver, the dinner plates, perhaps a salad bowl, and the wine glasses. Obviously, you shouldn't expect Grandmother's 12-foot dining table on a sailboat of this size, but you should look for a dining table that will allow three or four persons to sit in relative comfort as they partake of their culinary delights. If you can manage in a typical restaurant booth for four, you should expect to be content with your sailboat dining arrangements.

Some years ago, dinette (or dining) areas were mostly the afterthoughts of the folks who designed these sailboats. Back then, dining tables were designed mostly as platforms which could be converted into really uncomfortable "double berths." Not so today. The dining tables on most sailboats in the 22- to 26-foot range can actually be used for sitting down and enjoying a meal, even in relative comfort. Nevertheless, there are a number of things you should consider when looking at the dining facilities on a trailerable sailboat.

Size of the Surface

You need a dining table with enough surface area to set the table properly. Although this may be obvious to you, it isn't always as obvious to the sailboat manufacturers. Some boats have dining tables that fold down from a bulkhead and are long, narrow things—sort of like an ironing board. You don't want to try to eat on them. If you like everything else about the boat, however, you probably can find a way to increase the available dining surface.

Knee Room

Sit down at the table and make certain that it rises sufficiently high for you to get your knees under it. If you are not tall and your knees go easily under the table, stop and think about guests you may have onboard. Will they be able to get their knees under the table, too?

Stability of the Table

If the dinette hooks into a bulkhead or rests on a surface at one end with a single leg in the center near the opposite end, check and see if it is stable. Go to the end of the table nearest the leg and press down on a corner. If the table rocks, look and see if there is a way to keep it from doing so. I know that this was a problem on my Catalina 22, but it was easily solved.

Seats and Back Rests

Check out the seats and backs on the settees to be used when eating. Try to satisfy yourself that you will be reasonably comfortable while sitting there and that you will be able to reach your food without having to stretch halfway across the cabin.

Lighting

Just a brief note about lighting. It helps a lot if there is sufficient light for folks to be able to see what they are eating.

I don't know what you might be having for dinner. Maybe dinner is a pasta salad with some asparagus spears you have kept on ice. Perhaps you have grilled a steak and roasted a potato on the grill mounted on the sternrail. Whatever it is, you sit down in the warm glow of your cabin and light a candle at the dining table. Both the light and the music are gentle and soft, just like the sea lapping at the hull. There is a brief moment of silence and a passing seabird announces that it, too, is ready to dine. I can taste it now.

➢ CABIN WINDOW CURTAINS ≺

Window curtains for the cabin are usually optional. They give the interior a finished, almost tailored look but this is an expensive option. If you don't want to pay for what the manufacturer has available, there are a number of different kits, from metal rods to Velcro stick-ups, which will permit you to make your own curtains and hang them yourself.

Regardless of how you do it, I recommend that you have curtains on your cabin windows. It is nice to be able to go below and change from a wet bathing suit into some dry clothes without someone watching you through uncurtained windows. Also, at night with the cabin lights on, folks can see right into your cabin from a pretty good distance. Cabin curtains will also reduce the amount of direct sunlight that comes into the cabin, thus helping to keep it cool. Finally, if bright sunlight wakes you in the morning, you will need some curtains.

➤ PRIVACY CURTAINS ◄

What I have in mind here is some way to close off the V-berth area and the head from the rest of the cabin. In Chapter One I mentioned that the Catalina 22markII made some optional privacy curtains available to close off the porta-potti and V-berth areas. On my Catalina 22, my 18-year-old son would spend the night on the boat after a date with his girlfriend. Because Robert is a late sleeper, he would crawl into the V-berth and close the privacy curtains to keep out the morning sun. They worked well, and he would sleep until 10:00 or 11:00 o'clock.

If the sailboat you want to buy doesn't have these privacy curtains, I would recommend that you install them. It's easy and inexpensive, and you'll be glad you did some morning when you are reluctant to get out of bed. Speaking of beds, let's talk about sleeping accommodations.

➤ SLEEPING ARRANGEMENTS: BERTHS ◄

It has been a long day of sailing and you have covered about 50 miles down the coast doing some landfall navigation. The breeze has picked up significantly and turned directly across your stern as a thunderstorm builds directly behind you. The quiet little point at which you had planned to anchor for the night is in sight just ahead, and you decide to go wing-and-wing for the protection of the anchorage. The mainsail goes to port and the jib to starboard. Your sailboat responds immediately as the sails fill, while the sea behind you begins to boil into larger and larger swells, encouraged by the winds of the approaching storm. In almost no time you are there, pointing the boat up and dropping the sails. While your mate puts the sails to bed, you drop the anchor. No sooner are these tasks accomplished than the storm arrives. Both of you go below, put on some coffee, and wait for the foul weather to pass.

After an hour of thunder, lightning, wind, and rain, it is all over. You move into the cockpit with a cloth and dry off the seats. It's time to think about something to eat, and because it has been such a long day of sailing, you decide to fix something simple. After dinner it's a glass of wine, a cold beer, or a cup of coffee. The sun is well down now, and suddenly you are quite tired. It's time for bed.

You may be very different from me, but after a good, hard day of sailing I usually retire quite early and, as a result, arise almost with the sun in the morning. The reason is really simple—I have a comfortable berth to sleep on and I rest well. It hasn't always been so. I know, from personal experience, that there is absolutely nothing worse than to be ready for bed and to have one of those little coffin-like quarterberths to squeeze into and try to sleep. My bunk on the destroyer I served on in the Navy was more comfortable! I once spent five consecutive nights onboard a small sailboat sleeping in one of those tiny quarterberths. I was exhausted every morning. You don't have to be.

Here's what you do. First look at the thickness of the cushions on all of the berths. Cushions that are three inches thick are the minimum acceptable, while four inches of thickness is desirable. Next check the width of the berths. I have found that you need about 30 inches for one person and around 60 inches for two people. If it is a single berth, it will be no fun if one shoulder hangs off the side. If the manufacturer claims that the dinette converts into a double berth, find out if they mean a double for two small children, an adult and one child, or two adults. While we are concerned with width, let's examine the V-berth. I know it certainly looks wide enough; remember, however, that it loses width rapidly as it moves forward toward the bow of the boat.

Now let's look at the notion of length. I only know one way to make certain that a berth is of sufficient length, and that is to lie down on it in all three positions—back, side, and stomach. If you are six feet tall and you sleep on your stomach, your toes are going to extend another two to three inches beyond your normal six-foot frame. Make certain your berths can accommodate your method of sleeping.

One last piece of advice: when checking out a quarterberth that extends under the cockpit seats, make certain that there is enough vertical clearance for you to raise your knees slightly and turn over. If you can't, you will have to stay in one position all night, and that's agony.

Over the years the manufacturers of these sailboats have made significant strides in improving the comfort of the sleeping accommodations. I think you will be pleasantly surprised with the arrangements you will find available on trailerable sailboats in the 22- to 26-foot range.

➢ SUMMARY ≺

Let me encourage you to think of the cabin on your trailerable sailboat as your home on the high seas: you have a "kitchen," a "living room" or "den," a "bathroom," and "bedrooms." Admittedly, these areas are somewhat downsized on a trailerable sailboat, but they are, nevertheless, real definable spaces. If you are at all like me, you want your home to be as comfortable as possible. You will probably want the same for your sailboat.

5

The Challenges

There is no substitute for knowing your ship, its capabilities, and your own. There is no substitute for preplanning and practice, both for yourself and your crew. And there is no substitute for calm, rational action when an emergency arises.

TONY MEISEL, Nautical Emergencies

➤ INTRODUCTION ◄

Now that you have bought a trailerable sailboat, worked on the topsides, and checked it out belowdecks, are you ready to go sailing? The answer is no, not yet. First you need to know that sailing "big" is not necessarily the same thing as sailing "safe." You should never consider raising your sails until you are certain that you have done everything necessary to make it a safe voyage, no matter how brief or how long.

A common misconception about sailboats is that "bigger" means "safer." That is simply not true. Several people have crossed both the Atlantic and Pacific oceans in sailboats as small as 13 feet, or smaller. In fact, there are sea and weather conditions when a smaller, trailerable sailboat may actually be safer than a much larger sailboat.

Let me point out a few things for you to consider that give a smaller sailboat a safety edge. First, the sails on a trailerable sailboat are smaller and lighter and, therefore, easier to handle in heavy winds. Second, the mast and boom are shorter and lighter, and a broken stay or gooseneck will be easier to deal with. Third, there are not as many hatches to take on water in heavy seas, or in the event of a temporary knock-down. Finally, many trailerable sailboats are manufactured with positive flotation built in as an integral part of the boat. Simply put, compared to a larger boat, a trailerable sailboat has fewer things to go wrong. Furthermore, problems on a small sailboat tend to stay small and manageable. On the other hand, small problems on a big sailboat are usually bigger problems than big problems on a small sailboat.

To go sailing is to accept a challenge. It requires a willingness to place oneself in a competitive relationship with the wind, water, currents, tides, and other unseen factors which offer resistance to a sailboat's ability to go from one place to another. It is the sailor's task to harness these elements in order to sail safely to his or her destination. Sailing can be an exciting and rewarding experience, but it should never be undertaken without careful planning and preparation. Avoiding problems is not really difficult. As Des Sleightholme has suggested, "Keeping out of trouble is very largely a matter of thinking ahead. A chess mentality. Thinking ahead not only in terms of passage planning but in the small things." This is particularly true for the smaller, trailerable sailboat.

But don't let me mislead you about this, because most problems on sailboats have nothing to do with the size of the boat. On the contrary, the vast majority of problems are a result of mistakes by a skipper or crew—inattention, complacency, judgement errors, or a lack of sailing skills. There is absolutely no place for inattention or complacency on a sailboat, because both invite trouble. Human error can be reduced to a minimum by careful thought, advanced planning, and continuous practicing of sailing skills. In fact, thoughtful anticipation of trouble and repeated practice of solutions can make most difficult situations readily manageable.

➤ PHYSICAL AND PERSONAL INJURY ◄

In many respects, a trailerable sailboat is a finely tuned machine and, like with other such machines, things can break or go wrong.

Standing rigging can snap, your mast can crack, and the rudder can break. You can hit another boat, run into a submerged object, or an inattentive fellow boater can crash into you. Even if nothing happens to your sailboat, people on the boat can injure themselves by falling, or suffering cuts and abrasions. Sunburn is not uncommon, and the motion of the boat may make some people seasick.

Whatever happens—whether physical damage to the boat or personal injury or sickness affecting you or your crew, it is your responsibility to take all reasonable precautions to effectively deal with such situations, if and when they arise.

Equipment damage and personal injury can happen regardless of the sport or leisure activity involved. That's why people participating in sports wear pads, gloves, ear plugs, wrist bands, sunglasses, hats, helmets, and special shoes, to mention only a few items. The simple act of putting on your car seatbelt is an appropriate analogy to taking the necessary safety precautions. It simply makes good sense to have the right safety equipment on your sailboat.

In Chapter 6 we will talk about the safety items you will need on your trailerable sailboat so you can sail "big" safely. For now, however, let's talk a little about the most common ways a trailerable sailboat sustains physical damage, and the advanced planning and repeated practice you need to undertake to deal with them should they happen to you.

Being Hit or Hitting Another Boat or Object

There is absolutely nothing more embarrassing than running into another boat or object (such as a dock), and there is nothing more frustrating than to have another boat run into yours.

If you choose to participate in competitive sailboat racing, you should expect to experience a few bumps, bangs, and an occasional crunch from your fellow racers. This is particularly true when a large number of sailboats are jockeying for position at the race starting line. If, on the other hand, your sailing will be daysailing or short recreational cruises, your boat's bumps, nicks, and gouges will come primarily as a result of two situations: (1) you trying to leave or return to the dock and accidentally hitting another boat or object, or (2) another sailboat trying to do the same thing, and hitting your boat. Luckily, damage will usually be minimal in either case.

Let me tell you a little story that relates to what we are talking about. After sailing a 19-foot compact cruiser in total discomfort for three years, I reached the decision that it was time to move up to a Catalina 22, and to really begin to enjoy my overnighting and cruising. I brought my Catalina 22 to my home slip at the Tuscaloosa Sailing Club, put it in the water, and motored it around to my slip. Upon approaching the slip, I killed the outboard at about the same spot I did for my smaller and lighter compact cruiser. You can guess the rest. I had failed to compensate for the additional 1000 pounds of weight of the Catalina 22, and the momentum of the boat carried it right past the dock! If the Commodore and Vice Commodore had not been observing my seamanship, I would have crashed into the large rocks at the lake's edge. Both the Commodore, Wayne Townsend, and the Vice Commodore, Bob Dunn, helped me fend the boat off, and I narrowly avoided serious damage to the bow of my new sailboat. Wayne and Bob got a good kick out of my difficulty, and it was the topic of lively reporting and discussion for the next several days around the sailing club.

Here is some good, hard-learned advice on this subject. First, think! Think about leaving or entering the dock area before you actually do it. Second, plan! Plan your approach or departure before starting in or out. Many maneuvers require intelligent thought and planning on the part of the skipper; that is part of the mystery, the challenge, and the attraction of sailing. Third, practice! Practice maneuvering your boat in an area away from obstacles.

Sailboats do not like to back up, and they resist doing so by being reluctant to move and difficult to steer. Several things affect a sailboat's ability to move in reverse, including the shape of the hull, the location of the keel or centerboard, current at the slip, wind direction and velocity, and the outboard motor used to back the boat. These are things which you cannot change in any way, but you can most certainly take these elements into account and compensate for them as you plan your exit from the dock. For example, if you have a swing keel or centerboard, you can experiment with it at various positions to maximize steering control when backing. My advice is to take your boat out to some uncrowded water and practice backing up to see how the boat handles. Experiment by trying different tactics and you will develop a feel for how the boat reacts when moving in reverse.

Find out how the boat reacts to steering at different speeds. If you have a swing keel or centerboard, you will find that forward steering control is significantly diminished when the keel is completely retracted. That's because the keel serves as the pivot point. Again, experiment and determine how far the swing keel must be lowered to achieve good steerage. In addition, run the boat at the docking speed and see how far and fast it will continue to move with its own weight after the motor has been turned off. This will help you determine when you should kill the motor when approaching a crowded dock area and your slip. The last thing you want then is to be going too fast. Even if you don't hit another boat, you are liable to hit the dock, or go right past it and hit something else. A lot of sailors have suffered cuts, bruises, and even broken limbs by trying to fend off another boat or dock with their hands and feet.

Finally, it is a basic law of sailing that if you do crash into your slip, every "old salt" and/or member of your sailing club will be standing at the dock, smugly smiling as they watch you crash. *Think, plan, and practice, and you'll do just fine.*

Hitting a Submerged Object

A fairly common source of damage is the submerged object. Such objects can range from logs or stumps, to rocks, boulders, or very shallow islands on some inland lakes. Most of the time the collisions result only in scrapes on the boat's bottom, or perhaps gouges in the gelcoat. Occasionally, if the log, stump, or rock is of sufficient weight and mass, and if you are moving at a sufficient speed, the boat's bottom can be fractured or even holed. If this happens, you need to do two things. First locate the fracture or hole and determine if your bilge pump can handle the leakage. Second make some immediate repairs and assess your ability to return safely to shore without foundering. If you do have a reasonable doubt about your ability to return safely to shore, you must still undertake a repair effort and *use your VHF radio to notify the local authorities of your difficulty and request assistance.*

Basically, your repair efforts should center on minimizing the flow of water into the interior of the boat. I use the word "minimize" because you will not be able to completely stop the water coming into the boat. You can, however, slow it significantly. Here's what you do. First, locate the break in the hull. Second, if you have been holed, stuff the hole with towels or similar items. Once the cloth is saturated, the water flow will slow. If you have a piece of wood or other rigid object to fit over the cloth in the hole, do so, and try to brace it in place. You can also use some line and sailcloth to cover the hole from the exterior of the hull. The external water pressure will push against the sailcloth and form a pretty decent seal.

If the hull is cracked or fractured, try placing a piece of rubber or vinyl matting over the area, cover that with a towel and rigid object, and then brace it in place. Since the fracture was caused by an object striking the hull from the outside, the brace should help reclose the break and slow the intake of water.

Once you have the area sealed to the best of your ability, try to determine the proximity of the break to the waterline. If it is at or near the waterline, try moving everyone to the opposite side of the boat. The resulting heel may lift the break up and out of the water and stop the leak altogether.

Although you should worry about hitting submerged objects,

you shouldn't worry too much about it. The coastal waters of the U.S. are well-marked for hazards, as are the majority of inland lakes used regularly by sailboats. Just be sure to check the markers. The problem of submerged objects will be most common after heavy rains, with floating logs and other debris presenting the greatest hazard. Drought, on the other hand, can lower water levels and make previously harmless stumps, rocks, and islands more of a danger to your sailboat.

Many trailerable sailboat owners take advantage of the portability of their boats by taking them to new, distant, and inviting lakes. That's one of the true benefits of owning a sailboat you can hitch to your vehicle. When you arrive at a new lake, you should feel free to ask the local sailors about potential hazards. They will most likely fall all over themselves to tell you everything they know about local conditions on the lake and, as a result, you will have a safer sail.

Whether you are on your local waters or a new lake, know the effects of the weather, and take proper precautions. If you do, submerged objects shouldn't be a real problem.

➢ HEAVY WEATHER ≺

There is nothing more frightening than to be caught in truly heavy weather in a boat of any kind. To ensure your own safety and that of your crew and your boat, you should always check the weather forecast before leaving shore. If you are on a cruise, check the weather broadcasts on your VHF radio often to learn about approaching storms.

Storms represent the most significant danger to sailors, regardless of the size of the boat. This is true because winds can increase dramatically as storms approach or occur. As the velocity of the wind increases, so will the size of the sea in which you are sailing. In fact, the velocity of the wind and the size of the sea are the two factors you will need to deal with in heavy weather.

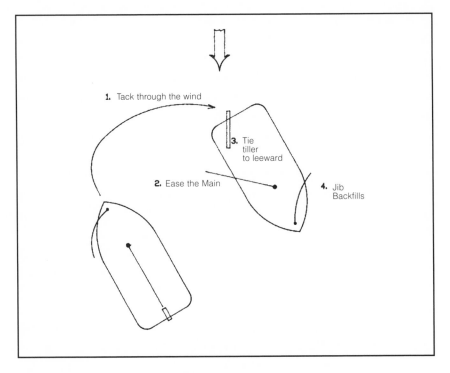

Figure 5-1. Heaving-to

Velocity of the Wind

The majority of your sailing will be done on days with a good sailing breeze of up to 16 knots (Force 4 on the Beaufort Scale of Wind Forces). When the wind starts to increase beyond this level, you should begin to think about reducing your sail area to compensate for the increased velocity, and to maintain adequate control over the sailboat. If you are sailing with a genoa for a headsail when the wind picks up, get it down, and change to a smaller working jib. Attach the jib and have it ready, but don't raise it yet. It is smart to have the sail ready, because if the wind continues to increase you may be required to raise the jib, and the foredeck area on a trailerable sailboat is not where you want to be when the wind and seas are up. Therefore, when the wind begins to strengthen, drop the headsail and go with the main. If your boat has a swing keel, you can adjust the angle of the keel to achieve maximum control when using the mainsail only. If the wind continues to grow, put a reef in the mainsail. Because it is already attached and you can do so without great risk, run the jib back up; when sailing with a reefed main, the jib will help balance the boat and give you better control. Here's where having your sail control lines leading to the cockpit is a real benefit, not only to comfort but personal safety as well. If the wind continues to build, you need to drop the main completely and try going only with the jib. When the jib alone proves to be too much to handle, you should either heave-to or drop all sails and run before the wind with bare poles.

Heaving-to is a procedure that can be used when the force of the wind and the size of the sea increase to the point that you are concerned with your ability to manage the boat while making any headway. Here's what you do. You are probably already sailing with the jib only, so raise your reefed main and ease it out. Without releasing the jib, tack through the wind so that the jib stays on the windward side of the boat and backfills. Push the tiller to the leeward side and tie it down. The pressure of the wind on the backfilled jib will force the bow of the boat down, away from the wind. Once the bow has fallen off the wind, the main will fill and the tiller lashed to leeward will force the boat back closer to the wind. Then, the main will luff and the backfilled jib will again force the bow down to begin the process over. Under this arrangement the boat will be balanced, and you will slowly wallow sideways. Heaving-to is no fun, but it will keep you upright and safe. Practice the procedure several times in light breezes so you will know what to do should it become necessary.

Rather than heaving-to, you may choose to run before the wind with bare poles. This entails doing exactly what the name implies—dropping all sails, turning the stern to the wind, and running with the seas. Because of its relatively light weight, a trailerable sailboat will ride along on the swells quite nicely. You will need to make certain that you do not gain so much momentum that steerage becomes problematic, so be prepared to drop a loop of anchor line or some other drogue over the stern to slow you down. You may find that the boat will surf along at a pretty good clip, so keep in mind that you will not be able to use this tactic in a small body of water.

Size of the Sea

Increasing wind causes the sea to build in size, and the bigger the swells grow the more difficult it becomes for a trailerable sailboat to manage to keep headway. Although light weight is an advantage when running before the wind, it works against you when heading into the sea. Large swells and waves will stop the lighter trailerable sailboat dead in its tracks, and nothing good can come from such a situation. In building or heavy seas you need to approach the waves at angles. When going down the crest of a wave point the boat off the wind a little, and when approaching the next wave, point the boat slightly upwind. Do not approach a large wave head-on because you will not have the momentum to continue, and once in the trough the next wave may push you sideways and knock you down. Ride a big sea at angles!

Because some storms develop very quickly, you may not be able to avoid being caught in bad weather. If thunderstorms are forecast, pay attention to conditions around you. If things look ripe for a storm to develop, take shelter and don't wait until it is on you to deal with it. I would rather listen to the "old salts" talk about surviving heavy weather than put myself, my family, my friends, or my sailboat in harm's way. Know about and respect the power of stormy weather.

➤ LIGHT WEATHER ◂

If heavy weather represents one end of the weather spectrum, light or calm weather represents the other end. In light weather there is no wind, or very little wind to move a sailboat along. Luckily, there are only a few days when there is absolutely no breeze. But there are quite a number of days when the wind is barely blowing, or the weather is "light." When there is only light air around, a larger, heavy-displacement sailboat has a real problem making headway without auxiliary power. Not so with a lighter displacement, trailerable sailboat! Because of its lighter weight, it will make headway when the big boys can't. I must admit, however, that when the breeze is really down, say one or two knots, headway will be difficult to come by. But you can help your sailboat gain forward momentum.

Here's what you do. First, minimize motion on the boat by asking everyone to be as still as possible. When there is very little breeze, pronounced rocking of the boat can spill the wind from the sails and stop all headway. Second, move everybody as far forward in the cockpit as possible. This will help get the stern out of the water and minimize drag. Third, examine your masthead fly and telltales to determine the direction of the breeze. Fourth, loosen the running rigging—boom vang, down haul, and mainsheet. You can even ease off the jib halyard an inch or two to give the sail some fullness. Fifth, ask everyone on board to move to the leeward side of the boat to create heel and capture whatever breeze is moving. Sixth, don't haul your sails in too tight. Light air requires relatively loose sails. Seventh, once you have some headway, steer gently. Remember, unnecessary jerks or rocking can spill very light air from your sails. Unless the breeze absolutely vanishes, you can probably make it back to your slip or mooring.

If what little breeze there is does disappear completely, drop your sails and crank the outboard. What the hell, you will still use less fossil fuel than the big boats!

➢ MAN OVERBOARD ≺

Perhaps Tony Gibbs said it best in his book *The Coastal Cruiser*: "There is almost never an adequate excuse for someone's falling overboard. It is nearly always carelessness, sometimes equipment failure, but it should not have happened." Although Gibbs is absolutely right, occasionally people do fall overboard.

If someone falls overboard from your sailboat, there is no reason to panic. Just remain calm and maneuver the sailboat to return and retrieve your passenger. Here's what you do. Stop the boat. If you are sailing upwind, tack and keep the jib backwinded. If you are sailing before the wind, round up into the wind immediately and let the sails luff. At the same time, throw the person overboard a flotation device—an "O" ring, horseshoe, or Type-IV buoyant seat cushion. If you are now alone on the boat, try not to lose sight of the person. If another person is still on the boat with you, have him or her keep their eyes on the person in the water. Tell them—emphatically—to do absolutely nothing else.

Now, with the boat stopped near the person overboard, you can begin your maneuvers to circle around and pick him or her up. There are a number of possible ways to maneuver for a man-overboard, and they all depend on your ability to handle your boat in difficult circumstances. It is extremely important for you to practice your routine so you will be familiar with it should the need arise. Throw a PFD out behind you and practice going back to retrieve it. Do it several times and it will ease your mind. It helps to know what to do, but there is no substitute for having actually practiced doing it.

Again, don't panic. Keep your eyes on the person overboard. And don't run over him as you come back to retrieve him from the water. It will be okay.

Let's pause for a moment and run a "reality check" on what we can do. We can get away from our slip without banging into other boats, the docks, or nearby piers; we can also return and tie up without crashing the boat. We can do a reasonably good repair-job on the boat if we hit something and begin to take on water. We can manage in heavy weather, and we can make the boat go in light weather. We even feel fairly confident that we can retrieve someone who falls overboard. Not bad! We are almost ready to buy our safety equipment. Before we do that, however, let's talk about two more possible events that happen to trailerable sailboats, at least every now and then, so you will have some idea of what to do if either event happens to you and your sailboat.

➤ BROKEN STANDING RIGGING ≺

Probably the most spectacular event that can happen to a sailboat is a dismasting. Unless you find yourself in weather so heavy that the standing rigging cannot absorb the loads, dismasting can be avoided with simple maintenance checks, and by taking proper care of the stays and shrouds when raising the mast. I say this because most dismasting problems occur because a stay or shroud breaks, and the mast comes crashing down as a result. If you do routine inspections of your stays and shrouds, examining them for broken wire strands, burrs, etc., you can minimize the possibility of breakage. In addition, be very careful not to kink the stays or shrouds when raising the mast. Kinks can weaken the wire strands that make up the standing rigging, thereby increasing the possibility that it will break.

Not all dismastings occur because of broken stays and shrouds. Some happen as a result of sheer stupidity. Here's an example:

Luck was with us, as my nephew and I sailed, along with three other boats, from Perdido Bay in Alabama down the Intracoastal Waterway to Redfish Point near Pensacola, Florida. It was a fantastic sail on a starboard reach with 10- to 12-knot breezes all the way. We arrived at Redfish Point just about dinner time. We dropped our sails and all the crews rafted up to recap the day and munch some goodies.

While we were rafting up, I accidentally raised the turnbuckle boots that covered the shroud turnbuckles on the port side of the boat. That's when I noticed that I had forgotten to insert the cotter pins that hold the turnbuckles in place. My heart sank to my stomach. If I had tacked at any time during the day, the pressure would have shifted from the starboard shrouds to the port side shrouds, and my mast would have come crashing down. Apparently, in my haste to raise the mast and put the boat in the water, I had neglected to check everything properly. I had been stupid and foolish. Only a steady starboard wind had saved my mast! Don't be foolish; check the rigging carefully to make certain everything is as it should be.

Now, let's say it is a wonderful, sunny fall day with a steady breeze of 18 knots. You are on a broad reach sailing down a lake. As you approach the end of the lake you come about to head back to your slip at the local sailing club. You uncleat the working jib sheet, push the tiller to leeward, and head the boat through the wind. As the boat comes around, the main fills and you haul in the new working jib sheet and cleat it. Just as the jib fills you hear a short "ping," and the headstay breaks. What do you do in order to keep the mast from falling backwards into the cockpit? Well, what you must do is act rather quickly, realizing that the jib will most likely hold the mast upright for a few moments. Turn the boat's stern to the wind and let the main out so the wind will keep forward pressure on the mast, holding it up. If you can grab the two broken ends of the headstay and effect a repair, do so. If the break is too high up, rig a line as high as possible on the mast and run it to the stemhead fitting. Ideally, you might have a spare jib halyard, spinnaker halyard, or spinnaker pole topping lift that could serve the same purpose. Keep your jib up, drop your mainsail, and motor back.

If the backstay breaks, you need to reverse the procedure by turning the boat's bow to the wind. Drop the jib and push the boom forward, trying to backwind the main. This will help the main sheet hold the mast upright while you undertake repairs.

If a shroud snaps, bring the boat around to put the broken shroud on the leeward side. Drop your sails and motor back under bare poles. Remember, take care of your stays and shrouds and inspect them often. If you replace them when necessary, dismasting shouldn't be a problem.

➤ BROKEN RUDDER ≺

Broken rudders usually occur as a result of hitting a submerged object and, occasionally, from running hard aground. Regardless of how it happens, when a rudder breaks all steerage is lost and you need to drop your sails immediately until you can regain control of your sailboat. The easiest thing to do is start your outboard motor and use it to steer the boat back to shore for repairs. If you don't have a motor, or can't get it started, you will have to rig a temporary rudder by using a paddle or some other piece of equipment you have on board. Once the temporary rudder is in place and you are ready to proceed, don't raise very much sail. Your emergency rig will not hold-up under great strain.

Let me advise you to equip your sailboat with a kick-up rudder. It will greatly reduce the probability of rudder damage by simply riding up and over most submerged objects you might encounter. If your trailerable sailboat does not come standard with a kick-up rudder, but it is offered as an option, buy the optional rudder. You will be glad you did.

Now that we have discussed the more typical emergency situations you might encounter on your trailerable sailboat, you shouldn't think that these situations happen every time you take your sailboat out, because they don't. If you think, plan, maintain, and practice, they will most likely never happen to you.

➤ SUMMARY ≺

Probably the most frequent cause of all accidents is complacency. After 25 years of sailing, I have learned that when the weather is in a foul mood, it seeks human complacency as its companion.

Sailboats require us to be in full control even at anchor. Perhaps it is in this sense of being in control that we find the essential attraction of sailing. I can imagine nothing more satisfying than being completely relaxed, with all of the senses on high alert. It is in just such a state that one is wide awake to life, and fully receptive to all of life's stimuli. I actually pity the poor sailor who is not confidently alert, and who is not prepared to deal with what is going on around him. He will not enjoy sailing for long. He will, I suspect, soon tire of the level of attention that is required, and will be happier simply turning an ignition and driving a powerboat.

In the final analysis, the best advice I can give you is to know your own physical and emotional limits, and to know and respect the limits of your trailerable sailboat. Simply put, don't undertake a sail that will stretch your ability, or the intended design limits of your boat. If you are going on a cruise, think about the risks that may be involved before you leave shore. Although you will not be able to anticipate every situation, try to be prepared as much as possible. You can deal with many problems if you will think, plan, and practice solving them ahead of time.

6

The Necessities

Ships, I may say, when not at sea, are always being fitted out or refitted or worked over in some way; they are never complete; work on them is never done, they are ceaselessly, relentlessly demanding, and if you waited until every job was finished you would not put to sea at all.

ANN DAVISON, My Ship is So Small

➤ INTRODUCTION ≺

Before you raise your sails, remember that everyone on board assumes that you have taken all reasonable steps to make the sail a safe one. Not only do family and friends on your sailboat expect this, so do the people on other boats around you, the marine police, and the Coast Guard. Making a sail a safe one requires that you have certain safety items on your boat.

➤ VHF RADIO ≺

You absolutely must have a VHF marine radio on your sailboat. Without a way to communicate, you are isolated in the event of personal injury, damage to the boat, or unanticipated bad weather. Always remember that as the owner/skipper of a boat you are personally responsible for the safety of the boat and the people who are sailing with you. This includes being able to stay in contact with the rest of the world.

A VHF radio on board enables you to call for help and also to hear others who might be in distress so you can render assistance.

Beyond that, it is nice to be able to talk with other sailors in the vicinity. For all of the peace and security VHF radios provide, they are dirt cheap. Don't put your boat in the water without one!

The choice of radios is staggering, both in terms of features and price. The different features available on VHF marine radios include the following: (1) the number of U.S., international, and weather channels, (2) the method of channel selection, (3) the type of channel display, (4) a hailing feature, (5) a scanning feature, (6) the ability to power up or down on selected channels, (7) the ability to listen to two channels simultaneously, and (8) waterproofing. Prices range from about $150 to $600, depending on the number of features. Let's look at each of the features separately.

For a small boat sailor, the number of channels available is not a terribly important feature. In any case, the fewest channels I could find on a modern VHF radio is 45 U.S. channels, with 9 weather channels. Unless you are sailing into Canada or in other international waters, this will be plenty.

There are essentially three ways to select a channel—keypads, rotary knobs, or up/down buttons. I prefer the up/down button, but I don't think one method has a distinct advantage over another.

I guess you can still find a radio without LCD channel display, but I certainly wouldn't consider it. I do recommend that the LCD display have backlighting so you can read it after dark. Another feature is a built-in "hailer" which will enable you to communicate with your crew or nearby boats. This feature is not really needed on a small sailboat.

The scanning feature permits you to scan up to five preselected channels, depending on the price of the radio. I don't think this is necessary on a trailerable sailboat. A power-up/down button allows you to boost transmission power on preset channels in case of an emergency. This would usually be channels 13 and 67. Almost all VHF radios come with this function, so you might as well make certain the one you install on your boat has it.

Being able to listen to two channels simultaneously is something I highly recommend. This feature is called a "dual watch" function, and it permits you to monitor channel 16 (the emergency channel which you are required to monitor anytime you have your radio on), plus another channel at the same time. Most VHF radios claim to be "waterproof" or "water-resistant," so ask for a "waterproof" radio. For about $200 you can get a radio with all of the features you will need for the type of sailing you will be doing.

You will also need an antenna and the necessary coaxial cable and connectors. Install your antenna high up on the mast, and make certain it has at least a 3DB rating. I recommend a mast installation because the VHF signal is mostly line-of-sight, which means it doesn't bend over the horizon. Clearly, the higher the antenna, the farther you can transmit and the easier you can receive.

An alternative to a fixed-mount VHF radio is a handheld model. Handheld VHF radios do not generate as much power, but over the last few years they have improved to the point that both have most of the same features, and a similar price. The least expensive model I could find has a maximum transmitting power of three watts, with transmit and receive on channels 13, 16, 22, 68, and 72, and it receives three weather channels. Having a handheld aboard as a backup is not a bad idea in case your fixed-mount radio fails. Handhelds come standard with a short "rubber-ducky" antenna. They can, however, be connected to a sailboat's regular mast-mounted antenna to increase their range.

In summary, let me repeat that you absolutely need a VHF radio on your trailerable sailboat. A radio can be important in getting help in time of distress, both for you and other sailors. Additionally, it is wonderful to have when sailing with a group of boats. Without a VHF radio you are not only sailing small, you are sailing dangerously.

➤ FIRST-AID KITS ◄

Do not buy one of those "First-Aid Kits for Boats" that you find in America's discount department stores. They are not what you need on your trailerable sailboat! What you will need is a first-aid kit to treat people for routine sickness or injury. In the event of something more serious, the first-aid kit is designed only for emergency treatment before professional medical care is available.

In addition to the basic items that should be included in every first aid kit, you should also personalize yours. You should include medical items that you, your family, or regular members of your boat's crew find to be particularly effective for them.

Your first-aid supplies should be kept in a sturdy and clearly marked container. In addition, it is important for everyone on the boat to know the location of the kit so it can be easily retrieved and moved to where it is needed as quickly as possible. Finally, you should purchase a good first-aid manual with easy-to-follow instructions. The manual and first-aid kit should always be kept together. (The recommended contents of a basic sailboat first-aid kit are listed in Appendix A.)

➢ FIRE EXTINGUISHERS ≺

The best way to prevent a fire on a sailboat is to keep things clean and orderly. This means that in addition to making sure that oil, gasoline, and other flammable liquids are properly stored, you should make every effort to keep the bilge clean and free of conditions that might contribute to a fire. If you are at all like me, you will be quite fastidious about keeping your sailboat shipshape.

A trailerable sailboat has fewer built-in potential fire hazards than a much larger sailboat that is loaded down with fuel and electrical systems. In addition, fire extinguishers on a trailerable sailboat will certainly be closer to the source of trouble than on a larger boat. Sometimes, however, fires do happen, and you should be prepared to deal with them quickly and effectively.

Fires are classified as Class "A," Class "B," or Class "C," based on the type of material involved. Class "A" fires involve ordinary combustible materials such as wood, paper, and cloth. These fires can effectively be extinguished by water, so have a bucket with a line attached to it handy for throwing over the side and scooping up water. Class "B" fires result from the ignition of petroleum products, grease, and similar substances, while Class "C" fires are electrical fires.

Fire extinguishers are classified according to their effectiveness on the different sources, as "A," "B," or "C" type extinguishers. Fire extinguishers for combating Class "B" fires are required by law on boats.

Extinguishers using a nontoxic, dry chemical are the most widely used on trailerable sailboats. These fire extinguishers are portable and quite inexpensive, two facts which account for their popularity. In addition, they are readily available at a variety of retailers and through marine products catalogs. A dry chemical extinguisher should be UL rated and Coast Guard approved, which means it must have a pressure gauge to show that normal gas pressure exists within the unit. These extinguishers are appropriate for Class "B" and Class "C" fires. You should be aware that when discharged, they leave a powdery residue which can be difficult to clean up.

A second type of extinguisher appropriate for a trailerable sailboat is a portable unit charged with Halon 1211. Halon 1211 is a colorless, odorless gas which is heavier than air. Because of its weight, Halon 1211 will sink to the bilge and be effective in that area of the sailboat as well as on exposed surfaces. Fire extinguishers charged with Halon 1211 are three to four times more costly than the dry chemical type. They do not, however, leave a residue and will not damage electrical equipment on the boat. Like dry chemical extinguishers, those charged with Halon 1211 are appropriate for Class "B" and "C" fires. You can also buy a small, palm-sized Halon unit for quick use in a limited area.

On a trailerable sailboat you need a minimum of two fire extinguishers with mounting brackets and I recommend three—one mounted in the cabin, one in the cockpit under a cockpit seat, and a palm-sized Halon extinguisher near the galley. Make certain they are clearly visible and easily retrievable.

Even though your sailing will not be far out in the deep blue water, a fire doesn't care where you are sailing. And it is just as difficult for a fire truck to get to the middle of the lake as it is for one to go offshore. Again, my best advice is to keep your sailboat clean and orderly. By doing so you most likely won't have to deal with a fire onboard.

➤ TOOLS ≺

Pick almost any convenient weekend and visit the nearest facility where trailerable sailboats are berthed or stored on their trailers. What you will immediately notice is that the skippers of the trailerable sailboats not sailing are busy caulking, screwing, tightening, loosening, hammering, sawing, sewing, mopping, washing, inspecting, and polishing their sailboats. It seems that when we are not sailing our boats, we are invariably tinkering with them. We simply can't seem to leave our sailboats alone!

Pay special attention to the various implements all of these people are using: screwdrivers, hammers, needle-nose pliers, slip-joint pliers, vice grips, socket wrenches, sanding blocks, drills, caulking guns, hacksaws, and wire cutters, to mention only a few tools. These people will be sewing sails and sail covers, inserting cotter pins, adjusting stays and shrouds, drilling holes, inspecting running rigging, rebuilding fresh-water pumps, and checking electrical systems.

What all this means, of course, is that you will need a basic tool kit on your boat; there is always something that needs to be done. I don't know why it is, but even if everything is working fine, sailors have an unusual compulsion to tinker with something on their sailboat. And, of course, you will need a tool kit to make repairs should something fail or break while you are sailing. It will be an important addition to the safety of your sailboat. A list of what you will typically need for repairs under sail is provided in Appendix B. You will, of course, soon have many more tools than those on my basic list. You will see.

➤ PERSONAL AND THROWABLE FLOTATION DEVICES ◄

What we called "life vests" some years ago are now called "Personal Flotation Devices," or PFDs. Regardless of what they are called, they are required by U.S. Coast Guard regulations. On sailboats of 16 or more feet, you must have at least one Coast Guard approved personal flotation device of Type I, II, or III for each person on the boat. I have been inspected by local marine police on several occasions while sailing on inland lakes. Each time I had to show that I had a suitable PFD for everyone on my boat. They were spot checks, and I'm glad I had the right PFDs on board. In addition, you must have at least one Type IV, "throwable" PFD on the boat. While you are required to meet these minimum regulations, I strongly recommend that you have one PFD for every berth on your boat.

Let's outline the four general types of PFDs and their characteristics:

TYPE I PFD. This PFD is intended for offshore use and is designed to turn an unconscious person to a vertical or slightly backward position, with his or her face up. It is preferred for the rougher offshore waters because it has the most buoyancy (20+ pounds) and, therefore, does the best job of keeping a person's face above rough waters. These PFDs are usually big and bulky and, as a result, they are not comfortable to wear or convenient to work in.

TYPE II PFD. Designed much like the Type I, this PFD is intended for near-shore use. The Type II PFD will also turn a person to the vertical or slightly backward position with his or her face up. Because it has less flotation, however, (15.5+ pounds) it is best for use in coastal areas or on inland lakes where swells and waves are normally smaller than offshore. Having less flotation, the Type II PFD is not quite as bulky as the Type I. It is, however, no joy to wear continuously, or to try to work in.

TYPE III PFD. While this PFD has the same buoyancy as the Type II (15.5 pounds), it is not designed to turn a person from a face-downward position in the water. These PFDs are the least bulky and most comfortable to wear. They are also the easiest in which to work while being worn.

TYPE IV PFD. This PFD is designed to be thrown into the water, as opposed to being worn. It is intended to be grasped by a person in the water to provide flotation until he or she is brought back aboard the boat. The most widely used Type IV PFD is the buoyant seat cushion.

Coast Guard regulations for PFDs require them to be the appropriate size for the persons wearing them. This means that children should wear, or have available, the size appropriate for their weight. Generally speaking, Type I and II PFDs are sized for adults (90+ pounds of body weight) and children (less than 90 pounds). Not only would an adult size be extremely bulky on a child, it might actually be so loose that it could slip off. Make certain you have the appropriate PFDs on board. I would strongly urge you to require small children to wear a PFD at all times.

If you are doing night sailing, your PFDs should have small flashlights and whistles pinned on them so that anyone who falls in the water can be spotted.

I could give you a long lecture about being sure to wear your personal flotation device when you are on the boat. I know that you probably won't do it, so at least let me strongly urge you to keep your PFDs neatly stored in a readily accessible place. In other words, don't stuff them down in a storage area with lots of other things on top of them. In fact, buy a separate container for storing your PFDs to keep them readily accessible.

Remember, the sternrail is an ideal location for an "O" ring or horseshoe buoy mounted in a quick-release bracket. Both the "O" ring and the horseshoe buoy are USCG-approved Type IV

PFDs. In this instance, sailing big and sailing safely easily complement one another!

➤ FLARES AND FLARE GUNS ≺

All sailboats over 16 feet in length are required to carry USCG-approved visual distress signals when operating in coastal waters. Even though you may never sail in and around the U.S. coast, state and local regulations may require visual distress signals on your sailboat. When not absolutely required by any agency, they are, nevertheless, something you should have on board.

Although there is a wide variety of visual distress signals available—from flags to electric SOS lights—the most widely used on trailerable sailboats are USCG-approved flares and flare guns. You should store them so they are readily available for use when needed. In some states a flare gun may be considered to be a firearm and, therefore, subject to licensing. Check local regulations to learn the requirements for your area. Flares and flare gun kits approved by the USCG are widely available and, happily, they are not expensive. Even if not required in your area, distress signals can provide a useful communication back-up should your VHF radio fail. It's a good idea to have them on your sailboat.

➤ SIGNAL HORNS ≺

According to USCG regulations, sailboats up to 26 feet in length must carry a bell, whistle, or some other device that can make an "efficient sound signal." On trailerable sailboats this requirement is usually satisfied with a compressed-air horn. Until recently, these air horns were charged with Freon, a gas which has proven to be harmful to the earth's ozone. Luckily, a sailor can now purchase and use air horns with propellants that are much less harmful to our atmosphere. Although they do cost a little more than the older type air horn, I suggest that you spend a little more money and do your part to preserve our environment.

➤ PADDLES ≺

Don't feel embarrassed by having a paddle on your boat. Just be thankful that a paddle can move you along if the wind disappears, you have lost your mast, or your outboard motor won't start. It won't be easy, but you can move a trailerable sailboat with a paddle. Just take your time and don't overdo it. Paddle a while, and then rest. You'll get there soon enough.

If it will help you feel better about it, remember that a paddle can be rigged as a substitute rudder if needed in an emergency. You need to have one on board.

➤ ANCHOR(S) AND LINE ≺

If your sailing plans even remotely involve overnighting, or if you have any notion of stopping in the middle of a lake for a refreshing swim, you will need a good system for anchoring.

Most 22- to 26-foot trailerable sailboats use a lightweight Danforth anchor. For sailboats in the size category we are concerned with, a Danforth anchor weighing between 8 and 12 pounds, with 10 to 15 feet of chain and 150 feet of 3/8-inch nylon or Dacron line should be adequate for normal anchoring. It would also be a good idea to carry a second, lighter-weight anchor for short breaks from sailing, such as lunch or a quick swim.

Anchoring is a skill that must be practiced if it is ever to be mastered. There are several good "how-to" books available which provide in-depth discussions of proper anchoring methods. Read one of these books before you try to anchor your sailboat. It is a fundamental truth, however, that you will not be able to anchor with real confidence until you actually do it. Practice your technique, and be sure to do so when guaranteed success is not important to your safety.

➢ BILGE PUMPS: ELECTRIC AND MANUAL ≺

You have probably heard the old saying that "nothing is as effective as a frightened sailor with a bucket in his hand." I strongly suspect that there is a great deal of truth to that statement. Maybe that is why there is no federal requirement for a bilge pump (or any bailing device) on recreational boats. Nevertheless, you will need a bilge pump on your sailboat. In fact, you need two—an electric and a manual pump.

Electric bilge pumps for trailerable sailboats are not very expensive ($75-$100), and are fairly easy to install. Bilge pumps should be mounted as low in the bilge as possible, and you should be able to gain access to the pump from the cockpit. In addition to an electric bilge pump, you should also carry a handheld (manual) bilge pump in the event water reaches your battery and shorts it out. For ultimate safety, have a good-capacity water scoop on board in case your manual pump also fails. Given the old adage about frightened sailors and buckets, it is likely that the water scoop will work just fine.

➢ EMERGENCY LIGHTS ≺

If you have a power failure when sailing, powering, or when at anchor at night, the U.S. Inland Navigation Rules permit you to use a light as a signal to other boats. It is advisable, therefore, to have a good handheld Halogen lantern on the boat in case you need to make other boats aware of your presence. The Inland Rules require that your use of the light is such that it cannot be mistaken for one of your normal lights, and that you not use it in a manner that disrupts the navigation of other vessels. In other words, don't shine a beacon into a wheelhouse, or into the eyes of another sailor who is steering a passing boat.

➤ BINOCULARS ◄

A good pair of binoculars should be basic equipment on every cruising sailboat, regardless of size. On a smaller sailboat, however, roll, pitch, and yaw will be more pronounced and there is a real need to enhance distance vision through the use of binoculars.

I advise you not to "break the bank" when buying binoculars. On the other hand, don't buy a cheap, useless set either. Try various binoculars before you purchase a pair. Ask the retailer to let you walk outside and assess their ability to improve your distance vision.

You can also walk around the marina and talk with the other boat-owners. Ask them about the binoculars they use (they will probably stub their toes hurrying to retrieve theirs to show you), and try them out. If they seem about right for you, get the details and buy the same kind.

The "power" of binoculars is given in two figures, such as "5 x 20," or "10 x 40." The first number represents the power of magnification, and the second number indicates the diameter of the front lens in millimeters. In buying binoculars, keep in mind that increased magnification equates to a smaller (more narrow) field of vision. On a 22- to 26-foot trailerable sailboat, binoculars with magnification numbers of "7 x 50" should be about right. Make certain the binoculars you buy are waterproof!

➤ CHARTS ◄

A chart is a nautical map emphasizing features which are of particular interest to boaters. It includes such things as the depth of the water, potential hazards to navigation, and the location and types of aids to navigation. In short, a chart shows features that will help the boater navigate the waters portrayed on the chart.

Charts are marked with grids defined by lines of longitude and latitude, set off in degrees. Within the grids, various land features, aids to navigation, and man-made features are represented through the use of various symbols. There are a lot of different symbols on a nautical chart—so many, in fact, that NOS (National Ocean Service) Chart No. 1 was constructed just to list all of the symbols common to all other NOS charts!

If most of your sailing is done on smaller inland lakes, you may not need a chart. However, if you sail on our larger lakes or around the coastal areas, you will need the appropriate chart(s) to navigate successfully, to know your location, to let others know your location, and to know where others are located.

➤ BOW PULPITS AND STERNRAILS ◄

I have talked about these accessories in a number of places, so I won't have a great deal to say here. Just let me remind you that these things can be real safety devices by helping to keep you on the boat. However, they will not be much help if you buy cheap pulpits and rails held together by pop rivets. The force and weight of a good-size person crashing against cheaply constructed rails will cause them to give way fairly easily. If poorly constructed, pulpits and sternrails may actually be more of a hazard than a help. In addition to being well constructed, they need to be correctly installed. They must be bolted through the deck with backing plates. Make certain they are not installed with self-tapping screws. If they are, you may hear a tearing sound when a lot of weight is placed against them—a sound that represents the screws giving way and tearing the fiberglass deck. If constructed properly, and installed correctly, pulpits and sternrails will be important safety features on your sailboat.

➢ EPIRBs ≺

An Emergency Position-Indicating Radio Beacon (EPIRB) is a low-power radio transmitter. EPIRBs are made to operate on lithium batteries that will make them work for two to five days when activated. The only type of EPIRB that could remotely be of interest to a trailerable sailboat works on the VHF radio bands by emitting a homing signal that can be picked up by aircraft that are in the vicinity. Because the EPIRB does not give the exact location from where it is transmitting, a fairly large search area is required to locate the user.

An EPIRB is a last-resort piece of emergency communication equipment, and should be used only when the boat is clearly going to sink. Actually, EPIRBs are designed for people who sail in the oceans, far away from land. If you clearly recognize and sail within the limits of your boat, they will not be needed on a trailerable sailboat. I recommend you do some in-depth reading before you make a decision to buy an EPIRB for your boat.

➢ SUNGLASSES ≺

Remember, only you can take care of your eyes, so make certain you have a good pair of sunglasses for sailing. Sailing sunglasses should absorb 100% of UV A & B, and offer excellent infra-red and blue light protection. Side shields that reduce ambient light intrusion would also be a good idea. Buying the right sunglasses won't be a cheap proposition, but they will be well worth the money.

Beyond the obvious need to protect their eyes from UV rays, sailors constantly have to deal with significant glare created by the sun reflecting on the water, on white decks and hulls, windows and windshields, and on sails, to mention only a few examples. Without good sunglasses, glare can cause impaired vision, and impaired vision is a hazard to safety. Get yourself some good sunglasses!

➢ RIP-STOP TAPE ≺

This tape is intended for emergency repairs to a sail should it rip or tear. It sticks to all fabrics and is very strong. In addition, it is waterproof. If your sail rips, this stuff will reduce the probability that it will rip even further and will, as a result, save you repair money. It is even inexpensive! Have some on board.

➢ SUMMARY ≺

It is difficult to talk about safety or safety equipment without making some people feel just a little nervous about undertaking an activity. I'm not sure that I can explain why this happens, but many people do have a tendency to get edgy, particularly when talking about safety on sailboats. Maybe it's because there has long been an air of adventure and mystery about sailing. Whatever the reason, I can assure you that ensuring safety on a trailerable sailboat is no more complicated or involved than making certain your automobile will take you from one place to another safely and securely.

7

The Amenities

To my mind the greatest joy in yachting is to cruise along some lovely coast, finding one's way into all sorts of out-of-the-way coves and rivers. A pleasant day's sail of four to six hours, and then, perhaps, a beat up some narrow, winding river.

R.D. GRAHAM, Rough Passage

➤ INTRODUCTION ➤

In this chapter we will discuss some of the amenities that add significantly to sailing comfort on a trailerable sailboat.

Often when I anchor for the evening I want to escape from my everyday life; the only thing I want to hear is the sound of silence. Sometimes I want to hear some good music and play cards or Trivial Pursuit with my family after a really good meal. Occasionally, I am on the water when my alma mater is playing an important football or basketball game, and I want to see it. I've found that a small portable television doesn't force the moon or stars to hide, the breeze to stop, or the birds to go away. I have one friend who reports watching his alma mater play football on television, while feeding the dolphins at the same time. Sounds like fun to me.

Let's take a look at the things we can add to our trailerable sailboat that will make it "bigger" and more comfortable.

Figure 7-1. Sun Shower   Figure 7-2. Shower enclosure

➤ SHOWERS ≺

People go sailing for a variety of reasons. We go in search of free-dom, adventure, and solitude. We go to commune with nature, to develop self-reliance, and we go in search of the unknown in dif-ferent and new places. Whatever our reasons, however, sailing puts us in a working relationship with the elements of nature, water, wind, and sun. Because most of us will do our sailing in the summer, we perspire and we get dirty. When we are sweaty and dirty, we look forward to getting cleaned up as soon as possible.

One way of getting fresh and clean is to jump over the side and use an environmentally safe soap. (I don't recommend this procedure when sailing in salt water.) Still, there is absolutely nothing that can compare to a refreshing shower after a long day of sailing. If you are daysailing and will return home or to the marina you departed from, or if you are sailing to a different marina at which you will tie up for the night, getting a shower won't be a problem. Today, most marinas have shower facilities available for people who use their slips. If, however, you plan to overnight on the water, or are on a cruise, you will need to plan to bathe on the sailboat. Although it will not be a four-star resort experience, you can have a shower that will lift your spirits and revitalize your energy. It may be somewhat novel and different if you're not used to showering outdoors, but you can take a warm shower and keep your body clean.

The Sun Shower, made by Basic Designs, is essentially a collapsible, "unbreakable" bag which is filled with water and is then set in the sun. The sun, of course, heats the water. After being in the sun for a while, the Sun Shower is hoisted aloft on a halyard or topping lift and the water is released through the shower head nozzle attached to the bag. Whenever I go sailing on the coast I see lots of these Sun Showers sitting on cabintops or foredecks in the full sun. I have used them myself and found that they work pretty well.

Sun Showers come in several different sizes with water capacities from 2.5 gallons, or enough for two showers, all the way up to 10 gallons, which is sufficient water for several showers. If you really value your privacy, you can buy a Sun Shower enclosure which is made of vinyl and has an inflatable framework. Also available is a "power shower" pump which you plug into a 12V cigarette lighter receptacle on your boat. Hook the Sun Shower hose into it, and you have a power-water system. You can purchase the whole system—Sun Shower, enclosure, and pump—for less than $75.00. The Sun Shower bag can, of course, be refilled and used over and over again. It's a neat little system and I recommend it.

➤ SCREENS ≺

I briefly mentioned the importance of hatch screens in Chapter 4 when we were discussing ventilation in the cabin area. In many respects keeping bugs and insects away is never going to be a totally successful endeavor, regardless of the size of the boat. Like the elements of nature, insects give not one damn about your wealth, power, prestige, or the size and cost of your sailboat. It will certainly be more of a problem on larger boats with several hatches than it is on a typical trailerable sailboat. More openings offer more points of attack for the little critters that want to bite and annoy you.

Frankly, your best line of defense is screens for your foredeck hatch and for the companionway, and the production model of your trailerable sailboat most likely will not have them. Making your own screens is really a simple matter. All you have to do is buy some mosquito netting from an army surplus or camping store, and cut it to fit your hatch opening. I sewed one side of some Velcro tape to the netting and outlined the hatch with the other side of the tape. The screen can be easily removed when I need to gain access to the foredeck through the hatch. You can make a similar screen for the companionway. Just be certain the screens attach from inside the cabin. If you don't want to mess with doing it my way, you can buy kits from the marine catalogs with everything you need. They will, however, cost you more and will not provide any more protection than the home-made screens.

I really don't like to put a lot of insect repellent on myself. I worry about all of those chemicals on my skin. But you know how mosquitoes and "no-see-ums" are—if there is just a tiny breach in your defense, they will exploit it and make you miserable. Because of this, I recommend that you do spray some insect repellent around the edges of your screens as a deterrent to the insects finding tiny cracks in your fortifications. If you have a pop-top cover, by all means spray around the edges of the cover where it fits loosely. In summary, take what precautions you can and know that those people on the 40-footer have a more difficult problem than you do. Good luck.

➤ SWIMMING LADDERS ≺

Imagine a warm Saturday evening at your local sailing club. Two Catalina 22s, a Hunter 240, and a MacGregor 26 motor out to the middle of the moonlit lake and raft up. The middle boat drops its anchor to keep the raft up in place. Everyone puts on a bathing suit and jumps into the water. The lake is supplied by a river and you can just feel the cool stream of river water as it moves past your body. After about an hour in the water everyone is cooled off and ready to return to the boats. You swim up to the boat and, looking up, see that the top of the transom looks as high as Mount McKinley. How in the world are you going to pull yourself out of the water, over the side, and into the cockpit? No problem, you say. Well, if you haven't tried to do it you have no idea just how big a problem it will be. This is particularly true for young children, and for older folks whose strength isn't what it once was.

I included swimming ladders as "amenities" only because they are optional equipment on trailerable sailboats. They are necessities, and I truly believe that every trailerable sailboat should have a swimming ladder mounted on the transom. In addition to making swimming more enjoyable, because you can re-enter the cockpit more easily, they are essential to have when small children are swimming or in case an emergency occurs. If you have to get in the water and use all of your energy pushing the boat off that sand bar on which you ran aground, it sure helps to be able to have a swimming ladder to reboard the boat.

Swimming ladders come in a wide variety of styles and configurations. You can get "hook-style" ladders that hook over the gunwales and collapsible ladders that attach to cleats. I don't care for either of those. What you need is a stern-mounted, fold-down ladder. The ladder should be all stainless steel, including the mounting brackets and the hinges.

➤ SHORE POWER ◄

Shore power will connect you to household current and voltage (110V AC) when you are tied up at a marina that makes this amenity available. You will need a power inlet mounted on the boat, usually on the side of the cabin or on the deck near the cabin. Once the power inlet is installed, wires of the proper gauge are run from the inlet to a household wall plug mounted inside the cabin. The power cord provided by the marina is plugged into your power inlet and, in turn, you can operate your carry-on air conditioner, onboard television, or other amenities.

The power inlet and associated parts can most likely be installed for around $200 to $250. If possible, I recommend you have your dealer install it before you take delivery of the boat. If you already own a trailerable sailboat, or your dealer cannot or will not do it for you, have the shore power connection installed by a professional. The potential hazards from a poorly or incorrectly installed power inlet are too great to risk having it done improperly.

I have not had a shore power connection on any of my previous sailboats. Instead, I bought a 100-foot outside extension cord and ran it from the nearest power outlet to my boat. I would then plug in a two-socket adapter and could run whatever I thought I needed. My thinking about shore power was that if my 100-foot extension cord wasn't long enough to reach an outlet on shore, I defined my boat as "out to sea" and not in need of the power.

Quite frankly, however, I did grow weary of having to look for a power outlet, running the extension cord back to the boat in a manner that would keep people from tripping over it, and having to find a place to store 100 feet of extension cord aboard when it was not in use. Really, what I disliked the most was being the only boat in my group without a shore power connection. *Felicity,* my new boat, has a shore power connection. You should have one, too.

➢ SOLAR PANELS ➤

Let's say you have invited one of your colleagues and his young son to go sailing with you. The three of you go for the day and find a quiet spot in which to anchor for the night. As dusk falls you go below to turn on the anchor light, only to learn that your battery has discharged to the point that nothing works. No interior lights, no fan, no radio, nothing! You don't even have enough power to illuminate your running lights so you can get safely back to the launch ramp or slip. Either way it goes, it is going to be an unhappy and embarrassing evening, and you are going to feel like you are sailing small. There is help on the horizon, however, and it is called a solar panel.

I don't want to mislead you on this subject and make you think that solar panels can serve as a power supply, because they cannot. What they can do is help prevent the unhappy situation of a drained battery cheating you and your guests out of a good time on your boat.

As sailors, we take great pride in the fact that our sport is in harmony with the elements of nature. It seems altogether fitting, therefore, that an ecologically sound accessory should have a place on your sailboat. In addition to their positive environmental status, solar panels have real practical attributes. They weigh almost nothing, make absolutely no noise, and are maintenance-free. Before you rush out and purchase a solar panel, however, let me give you a few caveats to think about.

First, an obvious truth—solar panels only work when the sun shines. Second, they are not cheap. Third, the output of solar panels is, in spite of real improvements in the technology, quite modest. If your battery is pretty well discharged, they will not fully restore its power in a 24-hour period.

Admonitions, disclaimers, and caveats aside, in my opinion solar panels are worth the substantial initial investment because they can and do make a significant contribution to increasing sailing comfort and decreasing potential inconvenience, embarrassment, and on occasion, real danger. Solar panels come in different sizes and with different capacities to recharge and/or maintain your battery. You need to keep in mind that the effectiveness of a solar panel depends on the brightness of the sun and the angle of the panel relative to the sun. Here are some examples.

Trickle Charger for an Unattended Boat

A five- or six-watt panel will generate between .30 and .40 amps, or roughly 2 to 3 amp-hours per day. On a sailboat left unattended for two weeks, a solar panel like this will restore about 28 to 42 hours of usage to your battery. A five- or six-watt panel is ideal for maintaining the charge on a battery that is exposed to the draining effects of heat in the summer or cold in the winter (usually between 5 and 10 percent a week even with nothing on the boat using power.)

Active Charger for Batteries under Fairly Light Loads

A 20- to 35-watt panel will generate somewhere between 8 and 17 amp-hours per day. On a trailerable sailboat cruising for a weekend on a lake or coastal waters, this solar panel will do an adequate job of maintaining the battery at an acceptable level given typical use.

Active Charger for Batteries under Medium to Heavy Loads

A solar panel rated at 45 or more watts will maintain a battery at peak operating power. In fact, it will do such a good job that you will need a system to prevent overcharging. Some of these high-wattage panels may actually be harmful to a 12V battery.

The power produced by solar panels increases with their size. West Marine Products offers the ARCO five-watt solar panel that measures 14" L and 14" W. The 20-watt panel by Siemens measures 22.4" L and 13" W, and the 45-watt panel is 42.6" L by 13" W, or a little over three feet long. That is awfully big for a trailerable sailboat with limited free surface area.

If your sailing is restricted to weekend cruises, you should stick with a solar panel of 20 watts or less. You are not going to be loaded down with ocean-going electronics, and your main concern will be maintenance of a sufficient charge on your battery for fairly short periods. I do recommend that you install a solar panel on your boat. It will ease your mind about the status of your battery and will make you feel better about using your VHF radio, stereo, fans, and other stuff. In addition, you can sail into a marina displaying the fact that you too operate on the cutting edge of technology!

➢ AUTOPILOTS ≺

An autopilot does not "pilot" your sailboat, you do that. An auto-pilot is actually an "electromechanical steering device" which simply holds a sailboat on a heading that you set for it. It has no effect on speed, it does not respond to changing sea conditions, and it cannot anticipate or react to danger. Until it is deactivated it will steer the course you tell it to steer, so you, or a designated member of the crew must be alert. It is not smart to engage the autopilot, set a course, and go below for an extended period of time. Doing so is simply inviting trouble.

If you have ever sailed in open water for several hours, you know how tiring long periods of time at the tiller can be, not to mention the problem of boredom and wandering attention. Relief from the tedium of extended periods at the tiller is one of the real benefits of an autopilot. Even if you haven't sailed for hours in the open water, you have most likely thought you were steering a straight course, only to look at your wake and discover just how crooked a course you actually did steer. An autopilot actually steers a straighter course than you can. In doing so it reduces both the distance and the time between two points of sail.

Autopilots are expensive, even those designed to operate on the tillers of smaller sailboats. You should expect to pay somewhere between $400 and $1000 for a tiller autopilot. Luckily, once you have decided you want an autopilot, they are not difficult to install. My advice is to consider the sort of sailing you will normally be doing. If most of your sailing will be for short periods on lakes, rivers, or bays, an autopilot may be too costly for the return in comfort it provides. On the other hand, if you will be involved in sailing that requires several continuous hours at the tiller, an autopilot may be just the ticket. It will certainly make your small sailboat bigger.

➢ CLINOMETERS ➢

Sailing clinometers are useful to have on your trailerable sailboat. For some reason a lot of sailors seem to think that the greater the angle of heel (tilt) on a sailboat, the faster it will go. We, of course, know that isn't true. We know that the boat sails faster if we can keep it as flat on its bottom as possible. That's why we continuously monitor the sails, letting them out until they begin to luff (flutter along the leading edge), and then trimming them in until the luffing stops, and no more. By continually adjusting and readjusting our sails, we keep the boat sailing as flat as we can in order to optimize speed.

Of course, a sailboat rarely sails perfectly flat on its bottom. It almost always leans to port or starboard under the influence of the wind. This is where a clinometer is useful. Technically speaking, a clinometer is any instrument used for measuring the angle of an incline. On sailboats, clinometers are small instruments which measure the angle of heel of the sailboat in degrees from the level position. They will help you determine the best angle of heel for speed and comfort for your sailboat. Different sailboats

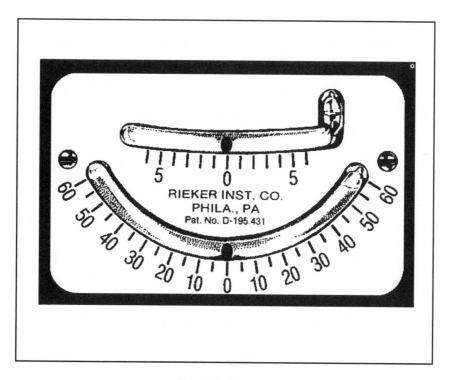

Figure 7-3. Clinometer

perform differently at various angles of heel. In addition, the same angle of heel may result in a significant difference in comfort on any two sailboats.

These instruments are not expensive, and are easily installed by any sailor. Just be certain you mount your clinometer where it can easily be read by the helmsman.

➢ APPARENT WIND INDICATORS ≺

There is a difference between "true" wind direction and "apparent" wind direction. If you are standing still on a dock with the wind directly on your right cheek, you are feeling the direction of the "true" wind at that spot. If you start walking forward, you will feel the wind shift slightly forward on the right side of your face. Now you're feeling the "apparent" wind, which is a combination of the true wind and the headwind you are creating by walking forward. In the same way, if you are sailing with the true wind directly across your starboard beam, the forward movement of the boat will shift the apparent wind slightly forward of the beam on the starboard side. Just how far forward the apparent wind will shift depends upon the speed of the true wind and the speed of your sailboat. Because sailors need to know the direction of the apparent wind, there are several ways to measure just where it is coming from.

You have probably noticed those little arrow-like devices located on the tops of masts, pointing in different directions as the wind shifts. My youngest son once told me they reminded him of jet airplanes without wings. Regardless of what such an arrow looks like, it is called a masthead fly. While the boat is sitting motionless at the dock, the masthead fly will point in the direction of the true wind; once the boat is moving, however, it points into the direction of the apparent wind and you use it to aid in sail trim. One of the most common of these devices is trade-named the "Windex." It is inexpensive and easy to install.

Telltales help you in determining the apparent wind and/or the airflow over your sails, depending on where you install them. Some telltales are attached to the shrouds on either side of the boat, using a rotating plastic disc to allow them to turn in the wind. These, like a masthead fly, give you an indication of the direction of the apparent wind. A second type of telltale attaches to the sail with a sticky disc. It will let you know how the air is flowing over the sails and help you maintain sail-shape for maximum use of the wind. For the amount of good information they provide telltales are very cheap.

➤ GRABRAILS ◄

If your standard sailboat doesn't come with teak grabrails (handrails), I strongly recommend you have them installed. This is particularly true if your boat has a traditional trunk cabin and you will be walking on the deck area between the side of the cabin and the gunwales. Grabrails are useful even when the boat is sitting in a slip, tied to a mooring, or at anchor. When they are sitting still with no wind in the sails to stiffen them, small sailboats can be fairly unstable. Just step from the dock to the gunwale of the boat and you will see what I mean—the boat will respond immediately to your weight and the gunwale will rock down and away from you. It's awfully nice to have some handrails to grab onto when this happens.

When you are out sailing and want to go forward around the cabin, grabrails are an absolute must for safety. Don't go out without them.

My advice is to install handrails that come as close to running the length of the cabin roof as possible. Be careful, however, and make certain that the handrails are not so long that they interfere with installing other things, such as turning blocks for running your lines back to the cockpit. Install grabrails made from teak wood, and not from metal. The teak will make your trailerable sailboat look much more expensive and will provide more of a finished look. I know that teak is hard to maintain, but nothing is better looking than well-cared-for teak on the exterior of a sailboat. You may cuss and fuss when you have to spend a few hours using a cleaner, a brightener, a sealer, and varnish on the handrails. When they are finished, however, they will look so good you will be proud.

➤ BOAT HOOKS ≺

No sailboat is equipped to sail big without a boat hook. I know from experience that halyards can work loose and fly up the mast and/or wrap themselves around stays, usually four to six feet beyond the reach of a fully extended human arm. Boat hooks are useful for retrieving wayward halyards and lines, snaring dock lines, and for picking up mooring lines. My advice is to buy a telescoping hook, one that expands to a minimum of six feet. They don't cost much, won't take up much room on the boat, and will save you a lot of frustration and embarrassment in front of other sailors.

➤ THE COMPASS ≺

A compass is an excellent safety feature on a trailerable sailboat. Although I prefer a permanently mounted easy-to-read compass, it is not essential that your compass be of that type.

The vast majority of small sailboat sailors will generally stay within sight of land, using "eyeball" navigation; i.e., relating what can actually be seen to landmarks and other aids to navigation displayed on charts. Nevertheless, a compass is an essential tool to help you get home should the weather become foggy or otherwise deteriorate. Let me give you an example.

One Saturday morning at the sailing club, our Commodore told me about a 40-mile sail he had taken on his Catalina 22. Apparently, it was fantastic, broad reaching with fair winds. After he arrived about dusk, he had a good meal and a delightful night on the boat. The next morning when he raised his sails to return, there was a slight mist in the air. Then, about 30 minutes out, the fog descended with great speed, and visibility was greatly reduced. The Commodore got safely home because he had had the good sense to plot compass courses on the chart for the first leg of his sail. On his return trip, he ran the reciprocals (direct opposites) of his original compass courses to stay on a good return course. He made it just fine.

Get yourself a functional compass and learn to use it. If you don't know how to use a compass, you can learn at home, without going sailing. If nothing else, have a handheld Boy Scout compass on your sailboat. Not only will you be able to find your position on a chart and get your boat and crew back to shore, you will be able to tell others of your location should you need help.

It is a basic truth that a 22- to 26-foot sailboat is simply not properly equipped if it does not have a compass. First and foremost, a compass is a navigational tool.

A good, permanently mounted compass costs between $100 and $200, depending upon the quality of the instrument. Compasses can be mounted in several different ways, on a bulkhead, flush with the deck, or with a bracket. Before you mount the compass you should give considerable thought to the idea of locating it for maximum ease of reading while in the cockpit. Also make sure to minimize the proximity of metal around the compass. Once installed, the compass should be checked for deviation, and then corrected.

You should buy a plastic cover for your compass. In addition to offering protection to the compass, covers make your boat look neater and better cared-for.

➤ DEPTH SOUNDERS ≺

One of the really great features of a trailerable sailboat is the swing keel, or centerboard. When the swing keel is in the fully retracted position, these sailboats can maneuver in very shallow water, allowing the sailor to slip into quiet coves and sloughs that larger boats simply cannot consider entering. The swing keel also minimizes the danger of running aground. If you do happen to run aground, and almost everyone does sooner or later, you can simply crank up the keel and get yourself off the sandbar or mudbank. On a 35- to 45-foot sailboat you must call for help or, if it's low tide, wait for high tide and hope your boat floats free. Of course, even with a swing keel, nothing good can come from hitting bottom with your sailboat. Depth sounders can be a real help in reducing this probability.

Like an autopilot, a depth sounder is not an inexpensive accessory. About the least costly instrument I have seen, and which I feel I could rely upon, is around $300. Most depth sounders I have seen are mounted just below the companionway entrance in an easy-to-read location.

You can buy depth sounders with all kinds of bells and whistles on them, but I think you really only need about four features. First, I recommend a depth sounder with an LCD digital display for ease of reading. Second, you need one that will respond to shallow water (preferably 1.5 to 2.0 feet), because you will be going places where bigger boats don't go. A depth sounder that starts at six feet is wonderful for a sailboat with a deep keel, but it is not particularly useful for a trailerable sailboat that has the ability to maneuver in 15 inches of water. Third, the instrument should have a feature which permits it to "look ahead" and sound an alarm when the water becomes shallow and approaches a preset depth you have selected. Finally, if you have a swing keel you probably will want to measure the depth of the water from your waterline. If, however, you have a fixed wing keel, you may want to measure depth from the keel. You need to buy a depth sounder that will permit you to do either.

A depth sounder is worth the investment if you plan to do any sailing in unfamiliar waters. Although this country does have a good system of coastal aids to navigation, the bays, sloughs, rivers, and lakes that trailerable sailboats frequently use are often poorly marked for shallow spots. You will be glad you installed a depth sounder the first time it prevents you from running aground.

➤ SAIL COVERS ≺

Your sails are what make your boat go, and you should take care of them. Most non-sailors believe that sail covers are intended to make a sailboat look neat and tidy. While they may achieve that result, they function primarily to protect your sails from the destructive effects of the sun and the weather. An uncovered mainsail furled on the boom, allowed to bake in the sun, flap in the wind, and broil in the humidity will soon suffer from a breakdown of the cloth fibers which make the sail. This is also true of the jib.

Sail covers are typically made from an acrylic fabric and are designed to completely enclose your sails to protect them from harmful ultraviolet rays of the sun and associated weather.

You really need sail covers to protect your investment in your sails. You should also consider getting a cover for your wooden tiller. These significantly reduce the probability that you will have to clean, sand, brighten, and varnish the tiller every season.

➢ MUSIC ≺

I had been daysailing in the Gulf of Mexico, just off Gulf Shores, Alabama, and was heading back through a small inlet to the Intracoastal Waterway, just as the tide had reached its strongest outflow. The winds and tide combined to create a really volatile sea. What did I do? After dropping the sails and starting the outboard motor, I did what any terrified skipper would do—I sent my nephew below to turn on the stereo, turn up the volume, and put a tape of Wagner on the cassette player. We forged ahead with unrelenting perseverance. With the strains of Wagner rising and falling to the crashing of the unhappy seas it was, to be sure, quite a ride.

After we made it into the Intracoastal, I killed the motor, we raised the main and jib and sailed smoothly away toward our anchorage for the evening. Following an 18-mile sail down the Waterway we arrived at Wolf Bay a little after dusk. While I set the anchor, Noel put the sails to bed and secured the mainsheet and tiller. It was a marvelous evening, with just a slight haze covering the new moon hanging in the sky.

As we settled in the cockpit, my nephew related his experiences at a concert he had attended just prior to graduating from Tulane University a couple of months before. I muttered something about rock concerts, went below, and put a tape in the stereo. That evening I introduced my nephew to Ahmad Jamal and his quartet's version of "Poinciana." As my nephew and I sat at anchor, drinking far too much beer, and waxing more philosophical with each passing hour, Ahmad Jamal performed with a brilliance that far exceeded all previous performances. It was an extraordinary concert on the water.

Your tastes in music may be quite different from mine. It doesn't matter. Until I had anchored in a quiet bay and listened to my own music, I had no idea of the serenity and peace that music can contribute to one's life. At night, after the breeze settles down and the sea becomes placid, the music surrounds you, and you hear notes and riffs you missed when ashore, with all of the noises attendant to living on land. Sailboats and music go together.

➤ TELEVISION ◄

At the beginning of this chapter I mentioned that I have been known to watch my alma mater play football while anchored. Normally, however, unless it is for an extraordinary reason, I don't feel comfortable anchoring in a quiet cove and watching TV. As a rule, it violates the essence of sailing. Now, let me hasten to add that everyone has their "extraordinary reasons," and having the tube on the boat is preferable to not having one.

There are a number of small portable televisions on the market today. They run from the really expensive to the not-so-expensive black-and-white versions you can get at discount stores. I don't think the manufacturers care about potential battery drain, so I wouldn't count on running one of these things off your marine battery. If you must have a television on the boat, get one that has its own rechargeable battery and plan to plug into shore power when tied up at the marina.

➤ DRINK HOLDERS ≺

There you are, it's a beautiful day with about a 12-knot breeze and you are on a port-tack beam reach down a long, uncrowded bay. Your daughter and her date are along with you for the sail. Looking around you notice two decent-size hills meeting each other along the starboard coast, about a half-mile ahead. The image passes from your mind as your daughter interrupts your thoughts and offers you and her date something cool to drink. A check of your depth sounder shows that the water is becoming shallower. You put your drink down on the cockpit seat to peer over the side, curious about the depth of the water. Then it happens, almost in a flash. You sail past the place where those two hills joined off to starboard. It seems that there is a little canyon between them and the wind comes rushing down the canyon, presses on your sail, and pushes it to port. The boat lurches to an opposite heel and your nice cool drink slides off the cockpit seat and dumps its contents all over the white slacks of your daughter's date. All you can do is control the boat, and apologize.

What you need to help deal with this and similar problems are drink holders that hang from lifelines or are mounted on cabin or cockpit sides. Drink holders will not solve all spillage problems, because sailboats can do some sudden lurching in strong wind shifts, or when plowing through rough seas. They will minimize the problem, however, and will make your leisure time in the cockpit more enjoyable.

➤ GRILLS ≺

The last few years I saw more grills hanging off the sternrail of sailboats than I had ever seen before. They were everywhere and they were in constant use. Not all of them were custom-made for boats. Some were what I once saw described in a sailing magazine as a "poor man's grill." The most innovative get-up was a flat-bottomed grill sitting on two metal rods that rested on the stern and extended out to the stern-mounted swim ladder. The ladder had been pushed about two feet away from the boat and was held in place by the weight of the grill and a line from the ladder back to the boat. It worked! I don't know how much the metal rods and the grill cost the owner of the boat, but I feel certain it was less expensive than a grill made for use on a boat. I still wonder, however, what they did with the grill and the rods when they were finished cooking and wanted to go sailing.

I prefer the kettle-type grills that are mounted on the stern-rail. Mounting it on the rail accomplishes several things—it places the grill over the water, it keeps it out of the cockpit space, and it keeps it away from children. Additionally, if you are tied up to a dock, a grill mounted on the rail helps keep the fire, sparks, and ashes away from the wooden dock and other boats. When tied up close to other boats, it's good to be a thoughtful neighbor.

You can buy rail-mounted barbecue grills for the sailboat that use either charcoal or propane as a fuel. I have both types at home for use on my patio, and after each use of the propane grill I always go back to charcoal. It's what I recommend for the sailboat as well.

➤ FLAGS AND FLAG STAFFS ≺

I think that a sailboat flying a U.S. Yacht flag, a Yacht Ensign, or other "dressy" flags looks neat and nautical. I plan to order a flag staff for *Felicity,* my new sailboat. Flag staffs can be mounted on the transom or sternrail. They are not expensive and are a nice way to dress your boat. Refer to *Chapman Piloting* for a good discussion of recommended flag size and proper etiquette for displaying flags.

➤ SUMMARY ≺

Some years ago I would walk the docks at marinas and stop almost exclusively at sailboats in the 35- to 45-foot range. I would walk right past the smaller boats, guided by the mistaken assumption that the owners of the larger sailboats sailed more frequently, and in more comfort than the people on the smaller sailboats. For some reason, I believed that only "large" could mean comfort and convenience. I was, of course, fundamentally wrong. I didn't know then what I know now, that you can sail in real comfort on 22- to 26-foot trailerable sailboats. You can keep cool, lounge around in comfort, light up the cabin, and keep clean. You can sleep in comfort, swim with confidence, and watch television or listen to some good music. You can grill out, know where you are going, and let an autopilot help you get there. You can know the depth of the water you are sailing or anchored in and, of course, you can keep in touch. In other words, you *can* sail big on a small sailboat.

8

Buying Used: Sailing Big and Saving Big

Cast out into the world of truth and compromise, the real search began. No longer was our guideline "what do you want in a boat?" Now it was "what do you refuse to do without?" The list of our requirements shrank to one-third its former length, and even those items were shuffled, reconsidered, and modified. Boats we would not even have looked at before were now seriously considered. But the sunset we were going to float off into had lost none of its allure. Only the floater had changed . . .

HERB PAYSON, Blown Away

➤ INTRODUCTION ≺

There are a lot of people who are put off by the idea of buying anything, a car, a boat, or an RV, if it isn't brand new. I don't understand these folks, but I sure know a lot of them. There are also a lot of people who simply can't afford to buy a lot of things unless they are used. And finally, there are many, many people who want to buy a car or a boat, but who are perfectly happy to save their own money by allowing others to first lose their money through depreciation. If you fall into one of the latter two categories, this chapter is written for you.

If I had insisted on buying only new sailboats, my sailing days would have been delayed by at least 25 years. The fact is that I have never owned a brand new trailerable sailboat. At first I couldn't afford to; later on I didn't want to. Even though I have never had a new sailboat, I have had very fine, well-equipped trailerables that I have sailed happily and frequently. You can too.

In Chapter One I gave you what I believe are eight good reasons for buying a new trailerable sailboat. While all eight of these reasons apply equally well to the used trailerable sailboat, six of them need a little reemphasis: availability, affordability, liveability, sailability, raceability, and cruisability. Let's take a brief look at how they apply to used trailerable sailboats.

First, consider availability. As I said in Chapter One, just three manufacturers—Hunter, MacGregor, and Catalina—have combined to produce over 55,000 trailerable sailboats in the 22- to 26-foot range. This means that there is a lively and competitive used boat market which, of course, is a real plus for potential buyers like you. Second, of course, there is affordability. Like automobiles, sailboats depreciate in value, some more than others. Unlike cars, trucks, and vans, however, most sailboats are not used on a daily basis and do not take the beating that urban and suburban driving exerts on vehicles. As a result, a well-maintained fiberglass sailboat has a much longer life expectancy than a comparably maintained road vehicle. I'm not trying to say that trailerable sailboats are not subject to wear and tear, because that simply isn't true. On the other hand, it is true that the fiberglass laminates used to build trailerable sailboats are almost indestructible. More than likely the fiberglass hull and deck will outlast all of us.

If you are careful, you can buy an older sailboat with confidence. The real bonus is that you can buy a used trailerable sailboat in the 22- to 26-foot range for a lot less money than you can buy a new boat of the same size. Like with a car, the greatest depreciation occurs during the first two years. Here are some examples showing the initial savings when buying a used boat.

The Sailboats	Price New	Price Used	Year	Initial Savings
Catalina 22	$11,900	$4,000	1977	$7,900
Hunter 23.5*	$15,990	$11,900	1993	$4,090
MacGregor 22	$6,590	$2,500	1982	$4,090
MacGregor 25	$8,990	$5,000	1984	$3,990
MacGregor 26*	$10,990	$8,500	1989	$2,490
Catalina 25	$15,750	$8,500	1979	$7,250

*Indicates a water ballasted boat

Some years ago I bought a used 1977 Catalina 22 for $4,000. The boat, which was then nine-years old, was in excellent condition. A new Catalina 22 would have cost $11,900, an immediate difference of $7,900. But the savings didn't stop there because my used sailboat came with the following equipment that wasn't standard with the new Catalina 22:

1. A trailer
2. A boom vang
3. A VHF radio and mast mounted antenna
4. A 7 h.p. outboard motor with gas tank and bulb line
5. A porta-potti
6. A two-burner stove
7. A mainsail cover
8. A tiller cover
9. Sailbags
10. Four PFDs
11. Cockpit cushions
12. Flare gun and flares
13. A paddle
14. Three fenders
15. A clinometer
16. A Windex
17. A tiller tamer
18. New interior carpet
19. Cabin curtains
20. Reupholstered cabin cushions
21. A fire extinguisher

If you take this list of equipment and consult the West Marine Catalog to calculate replacement costs, you come to an astonishing figure of about $5,000! Because it is a used boat we are buying and presumably the equipment is also used, let's be fair and reduce the value of all those extras by 50 percent, to $2,500. Add that to the initial difference of $7,900 between the price of the used boat and the price of the new boat, and you have a total of $10,400. If you want to do it the other way, you can say my $4,000 purchase includes $2,500 for the equipment and $1,500 for the boat. Either way you see the significant savings you can make by buying a used trailerable sailboat. What this also means is that you can often find used sailboats that are already well equipped for sailability, raceability, liveability, and, hence, for cruisability.

➤ MATTERS OF THE CHECKBOOK ≺

OK, you have decided that you want to go sailing, and you are going to do it the only way you can—on an affordable, used 22- to 26-foot trailerable sailboat. Now it is time for one of your tougher decisions. How much money can you afford to spend on a used boat? Be certain that you decide how much you are able to spend, and not how much you want to spend. If you are careful and keep this distinction in mind, you will find that you own the boat, rather than the boat payments own you.

Take a long, hard, and realistic look at your budget. You already know if your budget will not stand the expense associated with buying a new trailerable sailboat, not to mention the additional cost associated with equipping it. You need to figure out precisely how much money you can part with in a given year. If you have $5,000 available to spend in a year, you need to check with your lending institution to find out how much is required for a down payment, as well as the total payments each year. You may find that a used trailerable that costs $5,000 requires a down payment of 20 percent, or $1,000, and an additional $1,550 a year in monthly payments. That will take $2,550 of your $5,000 "sailing money" and leave you with more than two thousand dollars for insurance, maintenance, registration fees, gas and oil, and money to spend on your sailboat. Remember, you will have finished paying for your used sailboat long before the person making payments on a new boat that costs three to five times as much. One last comment on this subject—if you have the $5,000 in cash, you can often show the seller a big wad of green bills and reduce the price of the sailboat by laying the cash on the table. A large roll of bills may have the positive effect of encouraging the owner to take less, and it can save you a bundle in finance charges.

When you find a sailboat you think you simply cannot do without, you should hold onto your wallet or checkbook, take a deep breath, and think again. Be truly cautious, and don't overspend. This is important if you want to be happy with your used trailerable sailboat.

➤ GOOD USED SAILBOATS: HOW TO FIND THEM ◄

I have a friend who once owned a Catalina 22 which he had, over the years, equipped to sail really big. My friend kept his Catalina 22 at a sail club on a lake only twelve miles from his home, and quite often he would go daysailing or spend a weekend on the boat. In addition, two or three times a year he would load it on the trailer, drive to the coast, and go on three- or four-day cruises with his wife and daughter.

Unfortunately, on one of his trips to the coast the "bigger is better" bug bit him and he bought a 30-foot, fixed keel sailboat. Of course, he had to sell his well-equipped Catalina 22 so he could afford to buy his new 30-foot sailboat. Now he has a very expensive 30-foot sailboat that he sails maybe three or four times a year. The rest of the year he gets to pay $210.00 a month for a deep slip in which to keep his "bigger and better" boat. Now, on a typical weekend, he drives out to the lake twelve miles from his home and sadly watches the trailerable sailboat owners go sailing in the warm sunny breezes. Often, when he goes to the coast to sail on his 30-footer, his friends load their 22- to 26-foot sailboats on their trailers, drive to the coast, and go sailing with him. You guessed it, he rues the day he sold his trailerable sailboat. But take heart, because my friend's decision (and that of others like him) to "move up" to a bigger boat is a plus for people who want to buy a good used trailerable sailboat.

Regular Sources

Like my friend with the Catalina 22, a lot of sailors sell their smaller boats for a bigger one, and by doing so put a lot of good used trailerable sailboats on the market. You can find these advertised in newspapers, sailing magazines, sailing club newsletters, and lakeside and coastal marine bulletin boards. You can also walk the wharves and see sailboats with "For Sale" signs hanging from their bow pulpits. Any of these sources is a good way to begin looking for the type of sailboat you want and can afford.

Permit me, however, to offer one caveat—when you find the boat of your dreams, it is very important to know why the person wants to sell the boat, and to be sure you know the reason before you buy it. Usually people who want to sell their trailerables do so for one of four reasons.

Why Sellers Sell

First, let's talk about divorce on the grounds of irreconcilable differences. Some people buy a sailboat and soon find that their vision of sailing is not compatible with the reality; that is, they find that sailing requires too much attention and effort to be classified as consistent with their idea of a leisure activity; it has become too much work to be fun or relaxing. Because the majority of those who fall into this category usually make the decision to get out of sailing fairly quickly, they still have a substantial investment they want to recoup, and they are often not willing to make a really good deal for a potential buyer. Be careful of these sellers.

Second, some people, like my friend who bought a 30-foot sailboat, simply want to "trade up." If you can catch them after they have agreed to buy the bigger boat, and, therefore, when they really need to sell their smaller trailerable, you can often get a pretty good deal. A subset of this group is composed of those who want a newer version of the same boat and need to sell their older trailerable sailboat to be able to afford the newer one. I bought the nine-year old Catalina 22 I described earlier from a school teacher who found a newer Catalina 22 he wanted badly. He had really taken care of the older boat, and it was in great condition.

Third, some people unfortunately find that they are hard pressed for money because of temporary liquidity problems. I've been there. Let me assure you that you can often make a great buy under such circumstances. You should be prepared for anguished looks, misty eyes, and the wailing and gnashing of the seller's teeth, however, because most of these people really don't want to part with their beloved sailboats. They just have no choice.

A fourth group consists of sailors who have sailed their boats both long and hard. They have, as my son Jon says, "gotten all the goodie out of them." Their sailboats are simply tired and completely worn out. Stay away from them and you will avoid getting stuck with a trailerable that is too far gone to refit or reclaim.

Before we go on to talk about what to look for in a used boat, let me tell you one more way to identify and locate used trailerable sailboats that you just might be able to buy for a good price. This method will most likely take a little more time and effort on your part; it will certainly require that you be a little bolder. To illustrate, let me tell you a little story.

Abandoned Sailboats

Some years ago I had a position with a college in the mountains of Southwest Virginia. The nature of my job required me to make frequent trips to Richmond. Since I have never enjoyed the sameness and boredom of driving on interstate highways, I would often travel Virginia's excellent four lane highways to Richmond. As a result, I typically would travel the final leg to the capital on U.S. Highway 360.

On one late summer trip I noticed a 22-foot trailerable sailboat in the driveway of a home just south of the city of Richmond, and I made a mental note of it. A couple of months later I took the same route and the boat was still there, only this time the Virginia pines under which it had been parked had dropped their needles, and the boat was covered with brown straw. In the winter the snow had covered the pine needles and the trailer tires had gone flat. It was a shame.

Late in the following spring I came that way again. The snow had melted, the pine straw was now limp and matted, and it looked like some pine sap could be seen streaking down the boat's hull. I had seen enough! I turned around and checked the address and name on the rural mailbox. Later that evening, after I had finished my business, I found the telephone number I hoped belonged to the sailboat's owner. It did, and even though he had not thought about it, he was interested in selling the boat at a reasonable price. I didn't buy the sailboat, but I told a friend about it, and he did.

Here is another example. A few years ago I moved to Alabama and was lucky enough to become a member of the Tuscaloosa Sailing Club. In addition to 25 good slips, three pavilions, a beach area, a great club house, and good camping areas, the club has a very nice boat yard where members can keep their boats on their trailers. On my first tour of the club facilities, I drove through the boat yard and made a mental note of the boats parked on their trailers. Three years later, two of those boats had never been moved! They had been allowed to sit out there in the blistering heat and humidity of an Alabama summer, the torrential rains and winds of southern thunderstorms, and the occasional subfreezing winter temperatures. Tires had gone flat, trailers had rusted, protective tarps had torn and disintegrated, cockpit and hatch drains had clogged with debris, and of course, gelcoat colors had faded. I'm certain that there were wasp nests, ants, and molded and mildewed halyards as well. Most likely, the teak handrails had peeled, or been broken by falling tree limbs. For all intents and purposes, these poor sailboats had been abandoned by their disinterested owners.

As bad as all of this is, such boats may represent the chance for you to make a terrific deal on a sailboat to which you can give a new birth, and enjoy sailing in real comfort. Admittedly, looking for a used sailboat in this way requires more time and effort, but it can pay you back through significant savings if you finally find the right boat.

Before we go on to talk about what to look for in a used trailerable sailboat, let me give you a list of boats that are the most frequently offered for sale.

Most Commonly Offered Used Trailerables

Cal 22	Hunter 25
Capri 22	MacGregor 22
Catalina 22	MacGregor 25
Catalina 25	MacGregor 26
Chrysler 22	O'Day 22
Chrysler 23	O'Day 25
ComPac 23	Southcoast 22
Hunter 23	

➤ WHAT TO LOOK FOR IN A USED TRAILERABLE SAILBOAT ➤

Let's assume that you have looked at a number of used trailerables and located two in which you are really interested. Now it's time to pick up the telephone and arrange to take a careful look at them. Following is a list of the things I would want to examine. One final piece of advice: as you go through your inspection, it is a good idea to keep a separate list of any problems you identify. If you can estimate the cost of repairing or replacing these items, it may influence the final price you are willing to pay for the boat.

Checklist of Items to be Examined

1. Hull and deck
2. Standing rigging
3. Keel and rudder
4. Sails and winches
5. Outboard motor and motor bracket
6. Electrical system
7. Hatches and lockers
8. Bilge
9. Berths, settees, and cushions
10. Porta-Potti
11. Galley
12. Cockpit drains
13. Chain plates
14. Running rigging
15. Trailer

Hull and Deck

If the boat is in the water, you will need to put it on its trailer and haul it out. Take a long, careful look by standing at the front of the boat and sighting down the hull. Look for waves, patches, discoloration, and blemishes. Waves may mean that the fiberglass for the hull was laid-up in a less than high quality mold, and this may reflect on the quality of construction of the whole boat. Run your hands down the side of the hull to determine if it feels smooth and even. If you see any areas of discoloration, it may mean that the boat has been repaired in that area. That isn't necessarily bad, but you should get some explanation from the owner, as well as check the repair from inside the boat. While you are looking at the hull, notice any nicks and gouges. Don't expect used boats to be pristine, but do be suspicious of any large gouges that show signs of not being attended to properly. If the hull seems to be in good shape, it's time to climb up and take a look at the deck. It should look in pretty good condition. Next, take a walk around the deck to check that the surface is sturdy. This is particularly important in the area of the cabintop and on the foredeck. Any noticeable weakness may indicate water damage by seepage into the reinforcing materials in these areas, or that some very heavy object has crashed onto the deck creating hidden structural damage. This is a critical test because structural repair work in these areas can be quite expensive. While you are up there, check the care with which the deck hardware—winches, fairleads, cleats, etc.—has been installed. You will be able to spot poor workmanship right away, and this may be a symptom of a badly maintained boat. While you are on the deck giving the fittings a good inspection, it is very probable that you will notice "star cracks" in the gelcoat. A star crack is easily recognized by an array of small cracks that look somewhat like one of those starburst explosions created by fireworks. They usually are the result of some localized stress, such as someone falling against a lifeline stanchion. You can fill them with putty, but more than likely they will reappear. My advice is to not be too worried about star cracks in the fiberglass—they are pretty common on used boats and pose no real threat to the integrity of the vessel.

Standing Rigging

For our purposes, the standing rigging is composed of the mast and spreaders, the boom, fore- and backstays, and the shrouds (sidestays), along with the turnbuckles and swage fittings. First, lay the mast and boom on level ground and look to see if they both appear to be straight. Look for any obvious dents or other signs of misuse or neglect. Make sure that all of the fittings on the mast are securely fastened and don't show signs of fatigue; they should all be stainless steel. Finally, check the spreaders for bending or twisting, especially where they attach to the mast. If the overall appearance of the mast is good, take a look at the stays and shrouds. Check for broken strands and burrs. Be sure to examine the stays and shrouds where they enter the turnbuckles and attach to the mast because any sign of weakness here is bad news, and will more than likely mean replacing the whole thing. If you are operating on a limited budget, replacing stainless steel stays and shrouds can have a significant impact on your wallet. If everything looks acceptable on the ground, it's time to raise the mast and secure it in place. Once the mast is up, walk to the back of the boat and make certain that it is properly aligned down the centerline of the boat and doesn't have a gentle bend that could not be detected on the ground. Now, walk to the side of the boat and see if the mast is bent forward or backward.

Once you are happy with the position of the mast, grab the boom and slide it in. It should go in easily and the gooseneck should work smoothly. Hold the boom level and sight down it to make certain that your check on the ground was accurate.

Keel and Rudder

If the boat has a fixed or swing keel check it for dents, nicks, and gouges. Again, don't expect it to look like it did when delivered from the factory—just make certain that it looks reasonably good (not like it has been struck by a submarine) and that there are no glaring cracks or fissures where it meets the hull. If the boat has a swing keel, you will want to do some additional checking a little later when you put it in the water.

Now walk around to the stern of the boat and take a look at the rudder. If it isn't a fixed rudder (and it probably isn't) pull it out of its mounting bracket and examine the pins that insert into the mounting bracket on the transom, making certain that they are solidly attached to the rudder. While you are at it, make sure the rudder mounting bracket on the transom is in decent shape and securely in place. Examine the rudder to see if has been repaired from previous damage. The leading and trailing edges of the rudder should be free of any significant gouges. If it is a kick-up rudder, make certain it can be brought to the up position fairly easily, and that any position-holding device actually works. Where the tiller attaches to the rudder, make certain that the through-bolt is snug and has not wallowed so much that slack has been created.

If you are satisfied with the condition of the hull and deck, the standing rigging, and the keel and rudder, the boat has already passed a major test.

Sails and Winches

As you know, sails are the primary source of power for a sailboat. They are quite expensive to replace, so you need to make certain that they have received reasonable care and are in decent condition. This is really not too hard to do.

Take the sails off the boat and spread them out on the ground so you can get an overall impression of how they look. Check the reinforced areas at the head, the tack, and the clew. Now go along the foot, the luff, and the roach of the sail to see if there are broken or flayed stitches and, on the mainsail, be certain that you also look closely at the stitching around the batten pockets. Be sure to flip the sails over and look at both sides. Remember that this is a used sail, so don't expect it to look like it was just delivered from the sail maker's loft. After going over all of the sails in this manner, look for any areas of discoloration. If the owner has cared for his boat, he will have made every effort to remove stains in his sails. Finally, check the boltrope on the foot of the sail, as well as the slugs on the luff. If everything looks pretty good so far, take the sails to the boat and hoist them. What you are looking for at this point is ease of operation, i.e., the mainsail should be easy to install (bend on), and should slide cleanly up the mast when you tug on the main halyard. The same is true for the jib and other sails. While you have them up, take another look at them to see if you missed anything during your ground inspection.

Once you have completed an examination of the sails, you can turn your attention to the sail handling winches and the blocks mounted on the deck. If the sail lines are led back to the cockpit, there will be some turning blocks located near the mast, on the coach house roof. All you need to do here is to make certain that the blocks spin freely. Now give the winches a spin; they should turn freely without much effort. If one doesn't, the bearings may be worn, indicating a need to replace the winch.

Outboard Motor and Motor Bracket

With the boat on its trailer, the real test of the outboard motor will have to wait until you launch the boat into the water. (For a discussion of desirable specifications for the motor, take a look at Chapter 2.) If the motor is not on the motor bracket, I suggest that you mount it. This will allow you to get into the cockpit and see how well the motor bracket works. You should be able to raise and lower the motor fairly easily, and the bracket should lock in the up position for keeping the motor out of the water when under sail. Two final points: the mounting block on the bracket should be in good shape (not in several pieces), and the bracket should be resistant to lateral movement.

Electrical System

When you buy a used trailerable sailboat it is quite probable that it will have some electrical and electronic equipment that comes with it, and often this equipment has been installed by the owner rather than by the factory or an electrician. So the first thing you should do is enter the cabin and turn on the electrical panel. Then turn on the various systems: running lights, interior lights, VHF radio, etc. Check these out to make sure they are all working properly. If everything is working, I advise you to check the care with which the equipment has been installed. Make sure that wires are bundled neatly and routed in such a way that they are not exposed to accidental snagging and/or separation. A neatly bundled and routed electrical wiring system is good insurance against battery drainage and, more importantly, fire.

Hatches and Lockers

Simply check to make sure that the hatch covers are not warped or cracked, that they open and close easily, seat evenly, and that drainways are clear. Take a look inside the lockers for cracks, fissures, and discoloration. Discoloration may indicate the presence of standing water, and you will want to look in the lockers again when the boat goes in the water. If the boat has an anchor locker, you should make sure it's actually large enough to hold an anchor and rode. Finally, check inside the locker to see if a heavy anchor has been dropped, causing significant cracks.

Bilge

The bilge is the part of a boat located between the cabin sole and the bottom, where water sometimes collects. However, a lot of trailerable sailboats have no through-hull fittings, and you should check to see if the bilge is dry. Where would the water come from?

Berths, Settees, and Cushions

This is a quick and easy area to check. Lift up the settee and berth cushions and rub your hand along the top of the fiberglass seats and berths. They should be dry. Now look at the underside of the cushions for any water stains. If they have a lot of stains, or if the fiberglass tops of the berths and settees are wet, it could mean that water is seeping in at the hull-to-deck joint. If you do find dampness, you will need to ask the seller about it.

Porta-Potti

For the past 15 to 20 years, most trailerable sailboats have been manufactured with a space to accommodate a porta-potti (chemical toilet). Some older trailerables (like the older Santana 22) were delivered with toilets that are no longer legal. All you have to do here is to check that the toilet works, and that it is legal.

Galley

In the galley you need to check out three things. First make sure that the manual fresh-water pump works adequately. Second, check the fresh-water holding tank for leaks. Finally, if the boat has a galley that slides back and forth on runners, make certain the drain hose isn't bent, kinked, or leaking.

Cockpit Drains

This is another simple area to inspect. Check to see that the drains are clear and open. It would be nice if they had screens over them to keep large pieces of debris out to prevent clogging.

Chain Plates

Chain plates are the metal fittings at the sides of the boat to which the shrouds attach. They are important because when a boat is being sailed hard there is a significant amount of stress—upward pull—being transmitted from the shrouds to the chain plates. Imagine that you are sailing south in Chesapeake Bay. You are on a starboard reach in an 18-knot breeze. The boat is well heeled, and the port shrouds are nice and limp while the starboard shrouds are taut and strained. All of that stress on the starboard shrouds is being transmitted to the chain plates. Clearly a chain plate failure could be a real problem. Check the chain plates for elongation, wallowing of the through-bolt holes, and any other signs of fatigue. Chain plates can always be replaced, but the cost of doing so can vary widely.

Running Rigging

The running rigging consists of the various sheets and halyards used to raise, lower, and control the sails. You should give them a good visual inspection and satisfy yourself that they are in good shape. Frayed or excessively worn running rigging is unsafe and will have to be replaced, and that can cost you a tidy sum.

Trailer

A lot of trailer sailors spend hour upon hour maintaining their boats and largely neglect their trailers. That's a shame, because without a reliable trailer a trailerable sailboat is just as immobile as a large deep water cruiser. After you put the boat in the water, go back and take a close look at the trailer. You will need to look at four areas: the frame, the wheels, the wiring, and the boat supports.

Regarding the frame, you are not going to be able to X-ray the welds for cracks, so about all you can do is look at the welds and satisfy yourself that they look solid. Next, examine the frame for scratches, dents, and rust. A visual examination will tell you if any rust has been neglected for too long. If the frame looks solid enough, take the wheels off and make sure the seals are in decent shape. Now check and be sure the bearings are well packed in grease. Finally, give the tires a once over and satisfy yourself that they are roadworthy. Next, move on to the wiring. As best you can, make sure that the wires have not grown brittle from age. Follow them to their various destinations (lights, ground, etc.) and check for loose or corroded connections. If you see a section of bare wire without insulation, plan on replacing the entire section. It won't cost a lot and it will ease your mind. You also need to connect the trailer to the car's electrical system and make certain all of the lights work properly. Finally, if the trailer has bunks for the boat to rest on, make sure they are intact and don't show an unusual degree of sag. Should the trailer have rollers, make certain that they roll freely.

At last it's time for the fun part. It is time to go sailing. When you board the boat be certain to ask the seller to tell you about any sailing characteristics that are unique to the boat. Knowing any characteristics peculiar to the boat may prevent some inadvertent damage, and it could save you some unnecessary embarrassment after you are underway.

If the boat has a swing keel, you should check the cable as you winch it down. While you are sailing, keep your ears tuned to the possibility of hearing an occasional "thump, thump" sound in the vicinity of the swing keel. I hope you don't hear it, because it probably means that the through-bolt on which the swing keel pivots has wallowed out the keel. Such a condition is by no means terminal, but it will need to be attended to.

Before you raise the sails and head away, you need to start the outboard motor. Check that it shifts smoothly from forward to neutral to reverse, and vice versa. Throttle the motor up and make certain it holds its RPMs without you tending the throttle, then throttle it back down. It should perform well.

After you have been sailing for a while, it is time to make one last check. You should recheck inside any lockers that showed discoloration during your earlier examination. If they are still dry, it may be that rainwater has been the culprit.

SUMMARY

Now you can settle back and revel in the boat, the water, and the breeze. If you feel pretty good about the boat and are considering making an offer to buy it, everything now revolves around your personal enjoyment of the boat. And that, of course, is an intangible factor that must be weighed and settled in your own mind. If you have absolutely fallen in love with the boat and want to own it, don't get carried away and pay the asking price. Remember that list of problem areas I asked you to keep? At a minimum you should adjust your offer to cover expected replacement expenses suggested by the problem list.

If, on the other hand, the boat doesn't seem quite right for you, don't despair. Remember that there are lots of used trailerable sailboats out there, and you will find the right one. If you don't buy this boat, you have nevertheless completed a wonderful educational exercise, and you are wiser for it. Hang in there and keep looking. You will find your sailboat.

9
Epilogue

LESSONS LEARNED

SOME FINAL WORDS

I clearly remember the experience of my first night at anchor. It was spent on my 19-foot O'Day Mariner, appropriately named *My Turn*. I had departed from Pirates Cove marina in Alabama early in the morning, sailed Perdido and Wolf Bays, and then broad reached the Intracoastal Waterway to Redfish Point in Big Lagoon for my first overnight anchorage. Although I was tired after a full day of sailing and could not wait to fall into the quarterberth and go to sleep, it was not to be. There were, as it turned out, lessons to be learned. Not that I didn't go to sleep, it's just that every fifteen minutes the sounds of the night would suggest that "I had better check this out."

The first nudge came around 1:00 A.M., when a rather large vessel (surely the largest aircraft carrier in the entire world!) steamed by, and my little 19-foot sloop was greeted with the wake and swells attendant to its passage. I awoke to find myself sliding out of the quarterberth with my already sunburned nose heading directly for the centerboard trunk. Luckily, my appreciable body weight was more responsive to the force of gravity than to free flight, and I descended to the cabin sole prior to an unhappy collision with the fiberglass trunk. No sooner did I pull myself up than the little sailboat glided up a swell on the other side, and I was unceremoniously catapulted back into my quarterberth. This last event was completed only after my head had a short but memorable encounter with the mast-step compression pole running amidship of the cabin. I felt as though I were inside the tumbling drum of the clothes dryer at home.

Collecting my wits, I lifted the weatherboard, slid the companionway forward and stepped out into the cockpit. I suddenly felt how cold a fiberglass surface covered with moisture can be to your bare feet at one o'clock in the morning. Couple that with the fact that my cold feet slipped out from under me and my rear end, covered only by jockey shorts, found itself also becoming acquainted with the same damp and cold surface, and it is easy to understand my alarm when I failed to recognize, in even the slightest way, the place I had anchored. I thought I had broken loose and drifted miles away. In fact, the swells had simply combined with the breeze to rotate my little sailboat around the hook and I was actually still secure in the same anchorage. Still, I thought, I should go forward to check on the security of the anchor line. This I did, jamming my toes into the lower shroud turnbuckle on the way, and learned that the line was secure.

Feeling somewhat less salty than I had the previous day, I gave a sigh, returned to the confines of my little cabin, and lay down around 2:15 A.M. I went promptly to sleep and must have stayed that way for at most 15 whole minutes. Around 2:30 A.M. I awoke to the sound of "clang, clang, clang." I had not adequately tied down the halyard for the mainsail (or, alternatively, the restless halyard had noticed that I had dropped-off to sleep), and it was gleefully slapping against the aluminum mast. I lay in the berth for a few minutes, pondering the wisdom of getting up again. The playful halyard insisted. Having grown wiser now, I put on my shoes and exited the companionway. I struggled to the cabin top and relashed the halyard, returned to my berth and slept like a baby for about 30 minutes.

It must have been 3:20 A.M. when I heard "flap, thud . . . flap, thud . . . flap, thud . . . ." In the fog of sleepiness I had no idea what it could be. "Damn," I thought, "is it serious enough for me to get up again?" One nice thing, my shorts were already wet and my deck shoes were still on, so going out once more would require little physical preparation. I opened the companionway hatch, stuck my head out, and looked to the left. Seeing nothing, I turned to look to the right and as I did the mainsail slapped me across the face like a young lady who had just been insulted by some lecherous old man. It seems that the breeze had picked up somewhat and I had not put the main to bed properly. Much like our cat, Agatha, who wants the best spot on the bed, my mainsail had decided that if it were not resting properly, I should not be either. After muttering a few comments under my breath, I gathered up the sail and put it back to bed.

It's interesting how when you are focusing on the sounds of one thing you often block out the sounds of another. I don't know if that is the case, or if the loose tiller had simply stopped going "thud, thud, thud." At any rate, it didn't resume its rhythmic noise until I had returned to my berth and dozed for another 15 minutes. Obscenity laws prohibit me from telling you my true thoughts upon waking at 4:05 in the morning. Emerging into the night air once again, I lashed down the tiller. As I turned around to head back into the cabin, I looked up and saw a cloud smugly smiling back at me.

I climbed back into the cabin, turned on the lights, and lit a cigarette. My next reflex was to grab a pot, pour in some water, and warm it on the butane stove for some instant coffee. I now realize that I had chosen, without making a conscious decision, to give up my struggle with the elements. While the water warmed I pulled some orange juice out of the cooler and drank it. After the coffee was ready, I grabbed a cushion, went into the cockpit, and sat there sipping my coffee. It was then that I noticed that my little Mariner, the wind, and the sea seemed totally placid and content. It was about 5:00 A.M., and the rising sun could be seen on the far eastern horizon. I was fully awake. I had just completed my first night as a sailor at anchor and I was exhausted.

Before refilling my cup I checked the V-berth where my first mate slumbered peacefully. Mind you, this was not the curvaceous form of a sailor's fantasy, but the gangly frame of my fearless nephew who had gleefully accompanied me.

I made a silent vow, and it has remained so until now, that he would never know the trials I had endured that evening. I was, after all, an accomplished sailor!

As I look back on that first night at anchor, I remember it fondly for the lessons I learned which have made subsequent nights highly enjoyable. For anyone contemplating their first night at anchor, let me give you some hard-learned advice. Regardless of size, a sailboat needs to be put to bed properly before the skipper even thinks about resting. This is a lesson too infrequently written about and, therefore, usually requiring that the novice overnighter receive a constant lecture from the elements and the boat. I don't know this for certain, but I believe that even the most cautious of first-time overnighters must endure such a fate. It is necessary, I believe, for the wind, the water, and the sailboat to join forces to teach the uninitiated the important lessons of preparation and humility. You can prepare for these three, and you should. But they retain the absolute right to make your night pleasant, or miserable.

Now, after many years and many anchorages, I have achieved some peace with these three adversaries. But I still retire early and I still awaken early, usually before the sun arises. The difference is that now I awaken fresh, and the sight of the stars beginning to fade as they rotate in the sky, and the sun announcing the beginning of another ordered and stable day, gives me a sense of personal accomplishment and peace that can be found nowhere else.

Here is my advice. Sail for the day, anchor for the evening, and await instruction. My three friends await the opportunity to offer their lessons. Remember, however, no matter how foolish you think you look, no one else is there to see you. And that is precisely because you are actually doing something most people only dream of doing. Have fun!

➤ SOME FINAL WORDS ◄

In summary I have a few more bits of advice for you. It's your boat and it wants to do things your way. You know your lifestyle best. If you have little people, it quickly accommodates to eager, curious hands on everything, and fast-food cartons in the galley. It quietly intrigues teenagers. It accommodates the guys and a full-house dealt around on a lazy night of friendly competition. It's there for you when music, the pop of a cork, and quiet moments in a long lovely evening are in order. And finally, it's there for you when you need to be alone.

It will be what you make of it. Give yourself time. Most of us don't get it all at once. That's why winter evenings with catalogs are part of the pleasure—building anticipation through the cold for what we order and add with each spring's first warm wind.

Finally, don't limit yourself to one lake or marina. Pick yourself out one as home, and be comfortable there. But remember, your boat is designed to trailer, and nosing into new lakes for a weekend's pleasure is exciting and challenging. Wherever you are, there are new places that are reachable for a few days of getaway and exploration. You learn with each trip about people, about places, about your boat and about yourself.

Not too many years ago, sailing was perceived as being the exclusive property of the very wealthy. In fact, the perception was fairly close to reality, because small cruising sailboats less than 30 feet in length were simply not available to most people. Oh, you could buy small, open-decked daysailers, but affordable small cruisers were just not an option. Happily, the situation has changed.

With the introduction of the swing keel and, subsequently, truly affordable trailerable sailboats, sailing has become an activity available to anyone with a desire to know the joys and trials of living in harmony and competing with the extraordinary beauty and the impersonal forces of wind and water. To sail is to affirm one's independence, demonstrate one's personal competence, and renew one's soul. It is no wonder that sailing is one of the fastest growing leisure and competitive activities in the country. By reading this book you have indicated a personal interest in the sport of sailing. Knowing that, I can assure you that sailing is a pastime you will truly enjoy.

So there you have it. I'm going sailing. It's a beauty of a day, and I wish you could join me.

Appendices

Appendices

CONTENTS OF A BASIC SAILBOAT FIRST-AID KIT

MEDICINES

1. Aspirin, Tylenol, etc.
2. Antihistamines
3. Antiseptic for cuts and scratches
4. Motion sickness pills
5. Eye wash
6. Antacid
7. Laxative
8. Pepto Bismol
9. Antibacterial ointment

CREAMS, LOTIONS, AND SPRAYS

10. Bugbite lotion
11. Suntan and sunblock lotion
12. Petroleum jelly

13. Burn cream or spray
14. Muscle-strain cream

BANDAGES AND WRAPS

15. Small band-aids
16. Big band-aids
17. Big bandages
18. "ACE" bandages, with clips
19. Adhesive tape

APPLICATORS AND TOOLS

20. Cotton swabs
21. Cotton balls
22. Thermometer
23. Tweezers

APPENDIX

B

CONTENTS OF A BASIC SAILBOAT TOOL KIT

TOOLS

1. Pliers; slip-joint, needle-nose, and vice grip
2. Standard, slot-head screwdriver
3. Phillips-head screwdriver
4. Crescent wrench
5. Hammer
6. Hacksaw
7. Wire cutters
8. Hand drill and assorted bits
9. Files; wood and metal
10. Tape measure
11. Socket-wrench set
12. Spark plug socket set
13. Assorted nuts, screws, and bolts
14. Roll of good, strong wire
15. Needle and thread for sail repair

SPARE PARTS AND SUPPLIES

16. Spark plug
17. Shear and cotter pins
18. Rip-stop tape
19. Corks
20. Hose clamps
21. Electrical tape
22. WD-40
23. Silicone sealant

APPENDIX
C

YOUR SAILBOAT'S TRAILER

When hitched to the tow vehicle, your trailer is the one thing that gives you the freedom to "sail" down the highway to new lakes, rivers, and bays; it is also your personal ticket to unexplored coves, interesting new anchorages, and unexpected friends. It just makes good sense, therefore, to take proper care of your boat's trailer. Luckily, it's not hard to do.

Here are some simple suggestions for maintaining your sailboat's trailer in good condition:

1. Keep it clean. Hose it off frequently, particularly when it has been in salt water, but also if it is only used in fresh water.

2. Check it for rust spots. Clean them up as soon as they become evident, and have some rust retardant paint available for use after sanding the spots clean.

3. Check the wheel bearings often, and repack them just as regularly. It wouldn't hurt to keep some replacement bearings with you when on the road.

4. Make certain the tires are properly inflated. Always carry a good spare and make sure that it, too, is properly inflated.

5. Maintain the electrical wiring on the trailer. Keep all of the connectors clean, and repair any broken insulation. Carry spare light bulbs.

6. Check the boat-bunks on the trailer for cracks, breaks, or signs of fatigue. Maintain the bunk coverings in good condition.

Once you are on the road, plan to stop every couple of hours to check the trailer-to-vehicle connection. While you are out there, make sure the trailer lights are all working properly. It only takes a moment, and it will ease your mind.

One of the real joys of trailering your sailboat down the highway is to see the folks in the passing cars ogle and drool with envy as they watch you from their cars. Have fun.

NOTES AND CREDITS

QUOTES

Reprinted by permission.

Leckey, Hugo, *Floating*. New York: W.W. Norton & Company, Inc. 1982

Maloney, E.S., *Chapman Piloting*. New York: Hearst Marine Books, 1989

Nicolson, Ian, *Comfort in the Cruising Yacht*. Dobbs Ferry, NY: Sheridan House Inc. 1987

Griffiths, Maurice, *Round the Cabin Table*. Dobbs Ferry, NY: Sheridan House Inc. 1985

Meisel, Tony, *Nautical Emergencies*. New York: W.W. Norton & Company, Inc. 1984

Davison, Anne, *My Ship Is So Small*. Leatherhead, Surrey: Ashford, Buchan & Enright, 1992

Graham, R.D., *Rough Passage*. Dobbs Ferry, NY: Sheridan House Inc. 1985

Payson, Herb, *Blown Away*. Dobbs Ferry, NY: Sheridan House Inc. 1995

ILLUSTRATIONS

Photos: 1-1, 1-5, 1-6, 1-7 courtesy of MacGregor Yachts
1-2, 1-3, 1-4, 1-10, 1-11, 1-12 courtesy of Catalina Yachts
1-8, 1-9, by Doug Dukane, courtesy of Hunter Yachts

Figures: 1-1 courtesy of Catalina Yachts
1-2 courtesy of MacGregor Yachts
4-1, 7-1, 7-2, 7-3 courtesy of West Marine Products
2-1, 2-2, 2-3, 2-4, 3-1, 3-2, 5-1 by Donnie Cobb

Index

ABOUT THE AUTHOR

Jerry D. Cardwell was born and raised in the South. He served in the U.S. Navy before pursuing study in his chosen field of sociology. He received his undergraduate degree from the University of Alabama, a Master's degree from the University of Maine and a Ph.D. degree from the University of Utah. Throughout his life he remained vitally interested and active in his field, believing that, "If we are to understand who and what we are, the answer is found in the study of the dynamics of human interaction, not the study of the individual." In the discipline of sociology the theory is called Symbolic Interaction. He pursued it, teased it and was teased by it, his entire life. He was the author of several texts and numerous articles in the field of sociology.

He bought his first sailboat, a small Sunfish-type boat, during his last year of graduate school and began to learn to sail in the canyon lakes of Utah. I believe he loved sailing because it, too, is a tease and can be teased in exchange. It intrigued him and it challenged him. "Think about it, work hard at it, practice it, and you will know it; and that is the gratification."

For many years, he enjoyed his beloved Catalina 22, which was the inspiration for this book. His last sailboat was a 23-foot Aquarius. He bought it near Annapolis and trailered it to its home slip at the Pelican Marina in Elizabeth City, North Carolina. The Pelican was just what he was looking for, friendly people who love to sail, a bottomless coffee pot, comfortable tables and chairs overlooking the slips and, always, someone ready for a little conversation. After several trips to add supplies, adjust this and that, and welcome needed help to install a new radio and antenna, he went down to take her out. He apparently was pleased with her performance, he was not out more than a couple of hours. This was a look-see, get acquainted with the waters trip. He brought her safely in. I know this pleased him; it is always tricky with a new boat and a new marina. With two lines to tie, he suffered a massive heart attack. While it was much too early in his life, I cannot imagine circumstances more to his liking than a good day out and a boat secured for the night.

Jerry was married and the father of two sons. His is a very close family, and he is greatly missed.

Nancy L. Cardwell
Birmingham, Alabama
September 1997